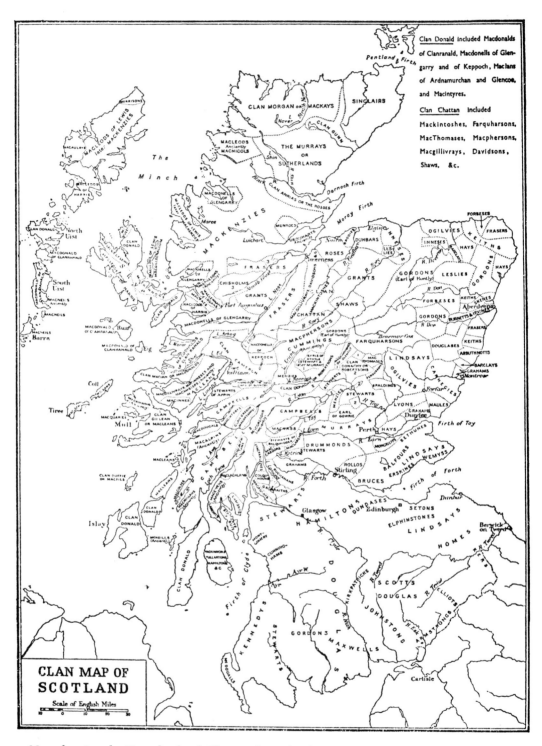

Map showing the Homelands of Clans and Lowland Families, from The Clans, Septs and Regiments of the Scottish Highlands *by Frank Adam (Famedram/Johnston & Bacon, 2004).*

Gathering the Clans

Tracing Scottish Ancestry on the Internet

Alan Stewart

 Phillimore

2004

Published by
PHILLIMORE & CO. LTD
Shopwyke Manor Barn, Chichester, West Sussex, England

© Alan Stewart, 2004

ISBN 1 86077 291 9

Printed and bound in Great Britain by
ST RICHARD'S PRESS
Chichester, West Sussex

Contents

Foreword
by Duncan Macniven, Registrar General for Scotland

The computer and the Internet have revolutionised the work of family historians. People researching Scottish ancestry are particularly well placed in this new electronic world. We have a good set of genealogical records: censuses stretching back to 1841 and registrations of births, marriages and deaths to 1855, parish registration (albeit patchily) to 1553, and wills (again patchily) to 1500. But, thanks partly to past efforts of the Mormons and others, and thanks more recently to investment by the devolved Scottish government and from the proceeds of the National Lottery, we have succeeded in making many of our records available on-line.

So, the evidence of Scottish ancestors can be brought into the living-room of anyone, worldwide, with an Internet connection, and into any public library or local family history centre.

Alan Stewart has written a powerful guidebook to this new adventure into Scottish genealogy. People starting ancestor-hunting will find here a clear introduction, and experienced researchers will find information on records new to them and familiar records in new forms. Last but not least, *Gathering the Clans* signposts forthcoming developments which will keep Scotland in its position in the forefront of provision for family history over the web.

DUNCAN MACNIVEN

Introduction

by J. Bruce Irving, FSAScot, Chairman of SAFHS

This book is a most welcome addition to existing publications on tracing Scottish ancestry because it focuses on *Internet* sources. It is particularly timely because in the last two or three years there has been an explosion of data available on websites that relate specifically to Scottish records.

This publication therefore complements the other books on Scottish ancestry that deal well with printed records and documents. Importantly it tells researchers how to access sources that have been hitherto inaccessible, or only accessible with difficulty, and also gives us a glimpse of records that will become available in the near future, such as those of the National Archives of Scotland and the Court of the Lord Lyon.

The range of information that is now available is extensive – almost bewildering – and it is pleasing to note that Alan Stewart has arranged it in logical order, thus making this compilation user-friendly.

There are bonuses too in the appendices, where you will find information on Scottish parishes and a map of Historic Counties of Scotland. These are particularly valuable to all genealogists, perhaps even more so to the huge number of people overseas who are seeking their Scottish ancestors.

For those with interest in a particular part of Scotland, there are website addresses for family history societies from the Borders to Caithness. These give access to local publications, and it is interesting to note that many societies and other bodies are now making them available on compact discs (CDs).

This comprehensive book is an absolute must for family historians, whether novices or the severely addicted.

BRUCE IRVING

Acknowledgements

Thanks first of all to Paul Parr, Deputy Registrar General for Scotland, who read through the whole book and offered a number of helpful suggestions. Martin Tyson, Departmental Records Officer at the General Register Office for Scotland (GROS), read and commented in detail on Chapters 1-3, and Hazel Anderson, Team Leader SCAN Testaments Project, looked at Chapter 4 and advised on the National Archives of Scotland's future digitisation plans. Thanks to them, and also to Elizabeth Roads, Lyon Clerk and Carrick Pursuivant of Arms, for information on the digitisation plans of the Lyon Court. Raymond Evans, Internet and External Services Manager at the GROS, helped with the illustrations for Chapters 1-3, and Paul Rowland, editor of *The Indiaman Magazine*, gave me advice about his databases. Thanks to them, and also to Bruce Irving for his enthusiasm and encouragement, and to Gary Beig of www. KensingtonHouseAntiques.com for permission to use the cover picture ('Gathering of the Clans') and a great deal of help in getting a suitable copy. In addition, thanks to those at Phillimore: Noel Osborne for being keen to publish the book in the first place, Simon Thraves for knocking it into shape (which I didn't always appreciate) and Nicola Willmot for creating the finished product. Finally, thanks to my wife Linda for putting up with me becoming more and more Scottish!

Illustrations have been reproduced with permission: Aberdeen & North East Scotland Family History Society, page 107; Clan Gregor Society, page 116; Commonwealth War Graves Commission, page 59; Dumfries and Galloway Family History Society, page 111; Family Research Link, page 123 (top); FFHS Publications Ltd (Online Division), page 124; Trustees of FreeBMD, page 123 (bottom); FreeCEN Executive Board, page 120; Genealogy by Genetics Ltd, page 114; General Register Office for Scotland (GROS), pages 5, 6, 7, 8, 11, 13, 15, 18, 21, 23, 24, 25, 27; GENUKI, pages 69, 135; Heraldry Society of Scotland, page 94; *The Indiaman Magazine*, page 55; Copyright © 1999-2002, by Intellectual Reserve, Inc., page 65; Copyright © 1999, by Intellectual Reserve, Inc., pages 66, 67; The National Archives, pages 50, 121; The National Archives of Scotland, pages 83, 88; Northern Books, frontispiece; Oxford Ancestors Ltd, page 113; Scottish Archive Network, pages 30, 130; State Records, New South Wales, pages 47; Tay Valley Family History Society, page 108. The map on page 135 is by Stephen Hew Browning and reproduced by permission of GENUKI. Some material in this publication is reproduced by permission of The Church of Jesus Christ of Latter-day Saints. In granting permission for this use of copyright material, the Church does not imply endorsement or authorisation of this publication.

Getting Started with Your Scottish Family History

INTRODUCTION

As a Scot, or a person of Scots descent, you have an advantage over everyone else when it comes to tracing your ancestors. The main records you need to look at to create your family tree have been made accessible over the Internet: birth, marriage and death records, census returns, and wills and inventories. There are websites where you can not only search the indexes to find these records, but also download digitised copies of the actual records themselves.

To get started tracing your ancestors, most books suggest you get as much information as you can from your elderly relatives. While I wouldn't disagree with that advice completely, just don't believe everything you're told. People won't deliberately mislead you (well, not usually): it's just that they may not remember very clearly what they were told when they were younger.

Take what you're told 'with a pinch of salt', use it as a pointer in (hopefully) the right direction, and check everything against the records. Beware of searching within a certain timeframe, because of what a supposedly reliable relative has told you (even if that person is one of your parents). He or she no doubt believes that a certain event happened at a particular time, but keep an open mind and widen your search if you're unsuccessful at first.

When you start recording the information you've found about your extended family, it's a good idea to make a note of your unsuccessful searches too. Record where you've searched, and back to what date. Otherwise, a few years later, you'll find yourself doing the same research all over again, either because you've forgotten you've already done it, or because you can't remember how far back you looked.

You'll probably want to use a family history program to record the information you find out about your ancestors: not only the basic details about a person's birth, marriage (if any), and death, as well as the names of his or her spouse and children (if applicable), but also information about your ancestor's life and career. Today's family history software lets you store photographs digitally too, as well as creating a 'family book' that you can share with your living relatives in print form, on a CD-ROM, by e-mail, or through your own website.

STARTING WORK ON YOUR FAMILY TREE

To trace your ancestors, you should start with yourself or your parents, and work back in time. When I started work on my family tree over 20 years ago, I began by sending away for the birth certificates of my parents, who were both born in 1911. If I were starting today, I'd still have to do much the same, as the Scottish birth indexes and records for the last hundred years are not accessible online, out of respect for people's privacy.

The marriage indexes and records are closed for 75 years, while those for deaths are closed for 50 years. (If you can get to the General Register Office for Scotland (GROS) at New Register House in Edinburgh, you can use the computerised system there to search the indexes and look at the records right up to the present day.)

According to the GROS's website (www.gro-scotland.gov.uk), there are four ways to obtain a birth, marriage, or death certificate. You can:

- Apply in person at New Register House, in which case you'll be sent a copy of the certificate within five working days. If you apply before 13:00, you can ask for a priority copy (at extra cost), which you can then collect at 16:00 the same day.

- Apply in writing, and you'll be sent a copy of the certificate within 10-14 days. If you use the priority service, the copy will be sent to you within one working day by first-class mail.

- Apply at the local Registration Office in Scotland where the birth, death or marriage was originally registered.

- Apply by telephone to New Register House using the GROS's Certificate Ordering Service (Telephone: +44 (0)131 314 4411). You'll need to quote your credit card number and expiry date.

The GROS says it can usually trace an entry in the statutory birth, marriage, or death registers, provided you give them the full name of the person, as well as the date and place of the event. If the person whose certificate you want has a fairly common surname, you should also let the GROS know the names of the person's parents (if you know them yourself).

The GROS will then carry out what it calls a 'particular search' (as opposed to a 'general search', which is when you do it yourself at New Register House), in which its staff will search for the record in the statutory registers (which go back to 1855) in the year you specified, as well as the two years on either side of it.

A Scottish birth certificate will give you the date and place of the parents' marriage, which you can then send for (or look up on the Web, if the marriage took place over 75 years ago). The marriage certificate will then give you the ages of the couple marrying, as well as the names of both sets of parents, including the maiden names of the mothers.

WHAT'S IN THE BOOK?

Using the birth and marriage records (see Chapter 1), you can work back through the generations of your family into the middle of the 19th century. Scottish death records are more useful than those of some other countries in that they tell you who the deceased person was married to (if anyone), the names of the deceased person's parents, the father's occupation, and the mother's maiden name (provided that the person who reported the death knew all that information).

Once you get back to 1901, you can start looking at the ten-yearly census records (Chapter 2), which let you see whole family groups of your ancestors, as well as telling you their ages and where they were born. Before 1855, you'll be looking at records of baptisms, proclamations of banns, and burials in the parish registers (Chapter 3). In addition, you can look at the index of Scottish wills and inventories (Chapter 4) to see if any of your ancestors made a will and, if so, what property he or she left.

In the second part of the book, you'll find information about other online indexes that can be helpful to you in tracing your Scottish ancestry. For those of you of Scots descent in the United States, Canada and Australia, there are several immigration databases and indexes accessible online (Chapter 5). I've also covered online indexes for those who served in the army (Chapter 6) or in the service of the East India Company (Chapter 7). The next chapter deals with online indexes for marriages of Scots abroad, those who fell in the two world wars, married at Gretna Green, or served in the police force (Chapter 8).

I then take a look at the FamilySearch online index to parish registers (and the first 20 years of civil registration), made available by the Church of Jesus Christ of Latter-day Saints (the 'Mormons') (Chapter 9). The same chapter covers the GENUKI 'virtual reference library' of genealogical information, and the Scots Origins website, as well as looking at various types of mailing lists and discussion groups. Then, for general information on life in Scotland at the end of the 18th and in the middle of the 19th centuries, you can read online the vivid descriptions written by local ministers in the Statistical Accounts of Scotland (Chapter 10).

I then look at records not yet accessible online, but which will be in the next few years. First of all, I consider the large number of records of various sorts (church, land, court, tax, and poor relief) held by the National Archives of Scotland (Chapter 11). Many of these records are currently being digitised, as are some of those held by the Court of the Lord Lyon King of Arms, who is responsible for Scottish heraldry, (Chapter 12).

The final part of the book covers a number of different topics, including the history of the Scottish people (Chapter 13), the various family history societies in Scotland (Chapter 14), how advances in genetics are affecting family history (Chapter 15), online access to indexes and some records in England and Wales (Chapter 16), and why it's a good idea to visit Scotland to see the country and research in the many local archives.

FAMOUS SCOTS AND THEIR ANCESTORS

Scots have long been interested in their ancestry. Scotland's greatest novelist, Sir Walter Scott (1771-1832), wrote in 1808 in a 'memoir of his early years' that,

> Every Scottishman has a pedigree. It is a national prerogative, as unalienable as his pride and his poverty. My birth was neither distinguished nor sordid. According to the prejudices of my country, it was esteemed 'gentle', as I was connected, though remotely, with ancient families both by my father's and mother's side.
>
> My father's grandfather was Walter Scott, well known in Teviotdale by the sur-name of 'Beardie'. He was the second son of Walter Scott, first Laird of Raeburn, who was third son of Sir William Scott, and the grandson of Walter Scott, commonly called in tradition 'Auld Watt' of Harden.

That other famous Scots novelist Robert Louis Stevenson (1850-94) wrote in a letter to his cousin Bob,

> You may be interested to hear how the family inquiries go. It is now quite certain that we are a second-rate lot, and came out of Cunningham or Clydesdale, therefore *British* folk; so that you are Cymry on both sides, and I Cymry and Pict. We may have fought with King Arthur and known Merlin. The first of the family, Stevenson of Stevenson, was quite a great party, and dates back to the wars of Edward First. The last male heir of Stevenson of Stevenson died 1670, £220 10 shillings to the bad, from drink.
>
> So much is certain of that strange Celtic descent, that the past has an interest for it apparently gratuitous, but fiercely strong. I wish to trace my ancestors a thousand years, if I trace them by gallowses. It is not love, not pride, not admiration; it is an expansion of the identity, intimately pleasing, and wholly uncritical; I can expend myself in the person of an inglorious ancestor with perfect comfort; or a disgraced, if I could find one. I suppose, perhaps, it is more to me who am childless, and refrain with a certain shock from looking forwards.

CONCLUSION

Now you may not be a famous novelist (or a famous anything-else), but like them, you and I and everybody has ancestors. Our ancestors may not be titled people like Sir Walter's, or be known as far back in time as the English King Edward I (1239-1307), who was called the 'Hammer of the Scots', and fought 'Braveheart' William Wallace and King Robert the Bruce of Scotland. Our perhaps less illustrious Scottish ancestors were alive in those days, however. They must have been: otherwise we wouldn't be here.

At present, Scotland gives you online access to more family history records than anywhere else, but let's hope that other countries follow its lead and put their official records on the Web as well. You can't do all your Scottish family history research sitting at your computer, but you can do a great deal, and in this book I've tried to put in everything I hope will help you trace your Scottish ancestry on the Internet.

Good luck with your research!

Part One

Records Available Online

1 Statutory Records (Civil Registration)

INTRODUCTION

On 1 January 1855, the post of Registrar General for Scotland came into being, with responsibility within Scotland for:

- registering births, marriages and deaths;
- looking after the Old Parish Registers, which had been used up to the end of 1854 to record baptisms, banns/marriages and burials in the 900-plus parishes of Scotland (see Chapter 3 and Appendix 2).

Later he was also made responsible for carrying out the decennial census in Scotland. Although civil registration of births, marriages and deaths had begun earlier in England and Wales (on 1 July 1837), the Scottish system was much more comprehensive, and therefore much better for tracing your ancestors, than that in use south of the border.

In fact, the registration system introduced in 1855 was so full of information that providing and collecting it was considered rather too much effort for registrars and informants. Unfortunately, from the family historian's point of view, some of the information (including, on the birth certificate, the parents' ages and places of birth, and the date and place of their marriage) was dropped in 1856. Fortunately for us, the date and place of the parents' marriage was restored to the birth records from 1861 onwards.

Until 2002, to be able to see the contents of the Scottish statutory records, you had to either travel to New Register House in Edinburgh, or send for certificates by post. As I lived in England, I had to carry out most of my family research by first consulting a microfiche copy of the Scottish civil registration indexes (at the Society of Genealogists in London), and then sending away for a certificate, using the reference number from the index. I usually needed the information on one certificate to be able to send away for the next, so this was a slow and fairly expensive process.

Now, however, you can sit in front of your computer anywhere in the world – in the US, Canada, Australia, New Zealand, South Africa, England, Wales, Ireland, or even in Scotland itself – and look up the birth, marriage, and death indexes online via the *ScotlandsPeople* website (www.scotlandspeople.gov.uk). You can then see a copy of the original record on screen, and print it out too. This is not only much quicker and easier than carrying out your research in the old way: it's much cheaper too!

ScotlandsPeople is the official government source of genealogical data for Scotland, and is a partnership between the General Register Office for Scotland (GROS) (www.gro-scotland.gov.uk) and Scotland On Line (SOL). SOL is a private company that provides Web-based services, such as internet access, website design and hosting, programming, and security services, as well as publishing travel and leisure content on its own www.scotlandonline.com website.

On privacy grounds, web access to the statutory records is restricted to births that took place over 100 years ago, marriages over 75 years ago, and deaths over 50 years ago. These limits roll forward with the passage of time, so that more births, marriages and deaths become available online each year. Unfortunately, to be able to look at more recent records, you still need to go to New Register House, where a computer system similar to the *ScotlandsPeople* website allows you to view the records using computers in the search rooms.

To use *ScotlandsPeople*, you first have to register with the site. This involves entering your name, postal address, and e-mail details via a registration screen, together with a username of your choice. You will then be e-mailed a password, which you enter, together with your username, to log in to the site. This takes you through to the 'Search the Records' screen, from which you can buy credits (see Appendix 1), and call up a specific search screen.

BIRTHS

To find a birth record, you need to call up the 'Search Statutory Register (SR) Births' screen. The only information you *have to* enter is the surname of the person you're looking for, but unless that surname is very unusual, your search would produce an unmanageable number of results.

Clicking on the 'search' button causes the search screen to refresh with an additional line stating how many index entries have been found. A search for 'Stewart', for example, produces a screen telling you that 52,865 Stewarts were born between 1855 and 1902, which could be displayed on 2,115 pages (at 25 names per page)! Searching for 'Saville', however, produces only 40 names on two pages.

Entering the forename as well as the surname is a start towards cutting down on the number of superfluous results, so that searching for 'Alan Stewart' produces only seven births in that same period. So far, this has cost you nothing. To see each page of your list of names, however, will cost you one of the credits you've bought. That's fine, when you only have one page to look at.

If I were trying to find the birth of my great-grandfather, William Stewart, however, I would find that 3,589 of them had been born between 1855 and 1902.

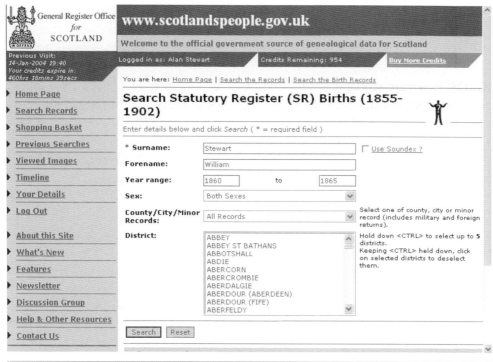

'Search Statutory Register of Births' page on ScotlandsPeople website.

To list them all would require using up 144 credits! It helps if you can cut down the range of years covered in the search. If I were aware from his marriage record or a census record that 'my' William was born sometime between 1860 and 1865, and entered that information, it would reduce the number of William Stewarts to 396 on 16 pages. That's better, but still a lot of credits to be using up.

Ah, but my William was born in the registration district of Thurso in Caithness up in the far north of Scotland. So if I were to select 'Thurso' from the list of districts on the search page, would that help? Yes, much better: there's only one William Stewart! So I can go ahead and click on the 'view' button, safe in the likelihood that this will be the birth record I'm looking for.

By holding down the <CTRL> key, you can select up to five districts for a search. If I didn't know the actual registration district, but only the county, then instead of selecting a district, I could choose the county of Caithness. My results page would then show that there were only two people named William Stewart born in that county between 1860 and 1865.

If I were to select a county with a large population of Stewarts, such as Perthshire, then I would find that this type of search wouldn't be quite so helpful, coming up with 46 Williams, which would display on two pages. In the City of Glasgow there would be 71 on three pages.

Web page showing number of records returned by a search in the Statutory Register of Births.

To see an image of the actual birth record of one of the people in the search results list, you click on the 'view' button, which will cost you five more credits. Another window will open on your screen, containing an image of the original page in the Register of Births with three entries, one of which will hopefully be the one you're looking for.

The information in the birth record will vary according to the year in which the birth was registered. From 1861 onwards the record shows:

- the child's forenames and surname;

- when and where he or she was born;

- the sex of the child;

- the forenames, surname and occupation of the child's father;

- the forenames and maiden surname of the mother;

- the date and place of the parents' marriage;

- the signature and relationship to the child of the person reporting the birth, and his or her address, if not where the birth occurred;

- when and where the birth was registered, and the signature of the registrar.

Criteria : Surname: "STEWART"; Forename: "WILLIAM"; Year From: 1860; Year To: 1865

No.	Year	Surname	Forename	Parent Name	Sex	District	County	GROS Data	Image	Extract
1	1860	STEWART	CHARLES WILLIAM		M	DINGWALL	ROSS AND CROMARTY	062/00 0009	View (5 credits)	Order
2	1863	STEWART	CHARLES WILLIAM		M	BLYTHSWOOD	LANARK	644/06 0636	View (5 credits)	Order
3	1862	STEWART	FRANCIS WILLIAM		M	LETHNOT AND NAVAR	ANGUS	300/00 0016	View (5 credits)	Order
4	1860	STEWART	JAMES WILLIAM		M	DALKEITH	MIDLOTHIAN	683/00 0114	View (5 credits)	Order
5	1861	STEWART	JAMES WILLIAM		M	PERTH BURGH	PERTH	387/01 0440	View (5 credits)	Order
6	1863	STEWART	JAMES WILLIAM		M	HUTCHESONTOWN	LANARK	644/10 1971	View (5 credits)	Order
7	1861	STEWART	JOHN WILLIAM GR		M	ST NICHOLAS	ABERDEEN	168/01 1225	View (5 credits)	Order
8	1865	STEWART	PATRICK WILLIAM	WILL	M	MENMUIR	ANGUS	309/00 0012	View (5 credits)	Order
9	1864	STEWART	ROBERT WILLIAM		M	PERTH	PERTH	387/00 0355	View (5 credits)	Order
10	1861	STEWART	RODOLPH WILLIAM		M	DUNDEE SECOND DISTRICT	ANGUS	282/02 1218	View (5 credits)	Order
11	1860	STEWART	THOMAS WILLIAM		M	HIGH CHURCH	LANARK	644/02 1437	View (5 credits)	Order
12	1860	STEWART	WILLIAM		M	DRAINIE	MORAY	130/00 0071	View (5 credits)	Order
13	1860	STEWART	WILLIAM		M	GAMRIE	BANFF	155/00 0032	View (5 credits)	Order
14	1860	STEWART	WILLIAM		M	RHYNIE	ABERDEEN	237/A0 0042	View (5 credits)	Order

List of results returned by a search in the Statutory Register of Births.

The information about the parents' marriage is extremely useful, leading you straight on to a search for their marriage record. It's only when you're trying to find the marriage of two people with common names in the records of a country like England or Wales – where a birth certificate doesn't give any clues as to the date and place of the parents' marriage – that you realise just how easy it can be to search for a Scottish marriage.

When the civil registration began in Scotland, a good deal more information was contained on a birth certificate. In 1855, in addition to all the information listed above, a birth record stated:

- the baptismal name of the child (if this was different from the registered name);

- the ages and birthplaces of the child's parents;

- the number and sex of the child's brothers and sisters, both living and deceased.

Unfortunately for those of us tracing our ancestors, this extra information, together with the date and place of the parents' marriage, was dropped from the birth certificate in 1856. It was felt that the registrars and informants were being

Page of records for Cambuslang in Lanarkshire from the Statutory Register of Births.

asked to do too much, and so their load was lightened. In 1861, however, the date and place of the parents' marriage made a welcome (for us, anyway) reappearance.

MARRIAGES

Finding a marriage record via *ScotlandsPeople* is similar to locating a birth record, only this time you call up the 'Search Statutory Register (SR) Marriages' screen. You have to specify the surname of at least one of the spouses, and if you also know the forename, you should enter that too. If you already have the birth record for one of the couple's children, then you'll know the year and location of the marriage, providing the child was born in 1855 or from 1861 onwards.

But what if he or she was born between 1856 and 1860? Unfortunately for me, my great-grandmother Elizabeth McIntosh Little was born in 1859, so there's no mention of the date and place of her parents' marriage on her birth record. Luckily, though, Elizabeth had a brother Andrew, who was born in 1864 and whose birth certificate states that his parents were married in Edinburgh on 23 April 1854. If only they had waited until the following year!

When you're searching for a marriage, because you have two sets of names to find in the index, specifying the district where the couple married is not so important. There were, for example, only eight marriages of a John Smith and a Margaret Brown in the whole of Scotland between 1855 and 1927, despite these being the commonest forenames and surnames in Scotland at that time. Smith and Brown may not sound very Scottish, but they're still the top two surnames (see Chapter 13).

Once you click on the 'search' button, the search screen will refresh with an extra line showing the number of records found. After clicking on the 'view' button on that results line, you'll see a screen listing the marriages that meet your search criteria. Click on the 'view' button for the marriage you think is the one you're looking for, and a separate window will open with the image of a page from the Register of Marriages. You'll see two marriages, one of which should be the one you want.

As with the birth record, the marriage record for 1855 contains more information than that from 1856 onwards. Although the record for 1856 to 1860 is laid out slightly differently, it contains essentially the same information as that for 1861 and beyond. This is:

- when, where and how the couple married;

- their signatures;

- the occupations of the couple, whether they were single or widowed, and their relationship (if any);

- the couple's ages;

- their usual addresses;

- the forename, surname and occupation of each father;

- the forename and maiden surname of each mother;

- the signature of the officiating minister and those of the witnesses (if it was a regular marriage);

- the date of the 'conviction', Decree of Declarator or Sheriff's warrant (if it was an irregular marriage);

- when and where the marriage was registered, and the signature of the registrar.

The names and maiden surnames of the two mothers are useful information that does not appear on (for example) English and Welsh marriage certificates.

The additional information on the 1855 Scottish marriage record is:

- the present addresses of the couple (if different to their usual addresses);

- if either or both of the couple were widowed, whether this was their second or third marriage;

- the number of living and dead children of the marriage partners by each of their former marriages;

- the birthplaces of the couple, and when and where their births were registered.

DEATHS

A Scottish death certificate is more than just a record of someone's death, as it also gives information on the deceased person's parents, which can take you back another generation in your family tree. Again, this is something that doesn't appear on the death certificates of England and Wales.

To search for a death record, you need to call up the 'Search Statutory Register (SR) Deaths' page on to the screen. While it's quite easy to go back in time from a birth certificate to the record of the marriage of the child's parents, and then back to the births of the parents with the help of their ages at marriage (and their places of birth taken from a census record – see the next chapter), searching for a death record can be much harder.

You may well have no idea how old the ancestor you're looking for was when he or she died. You may not have been able to find this person in the census. To assist you in locating him or her, *ScotlandsPeople* have put a 'birth year' box on the search page for deaths. This is helpful up to a point, but it does depend on the person informing the registrar of the death being aware of the correct age of the deceased person. You may well know exactly when the deceased was born: the informant may not have known this.

Having entered as much information as you can into the boxes on the search screen, click on the 'search' button. As with the birth and marriage searches, the page will refresh with a line showing the number of matching records. My own experience has been that, where you're trying to find someone with a name that's common in the area you've specified (or in the whole of Scotland, if you haven't selected a county, city or registration district), you may well have to view some 'wrong' images, before you find your ancestor.

From 1861 on the information on a death record is:

- the forename and surname of the deceased person;
- the person's occupation, and whether he or she was single, married, or widowed;
- when and where the person died;
- the sex of the deceased person;
- his or her age;
- the forename, surname and occupation of the deceased person's father;
- the forename and maiden surname of his or her mother;
- the cause of the person's death, the duration of the disease, and by whom the death was certified;
- the signature and relationship of the person reporting the death, and his or her address (if not where the death occurred);

1899. DEATHS in the Parish of Kirkliston in the County of Linlithgow — Page 20.—

No.	Name and Surname. Rank or Profession, and whether Single, Married, or Widowed.	When and Where Died.	Sex.	Age.	Name, Surname, & Rank or Profession of Father. Name, and Maiden Surname of Mother.	Cause of Death, Duration of Disease, and Medical Attendant by whom certified.	Signature & Qualification of Informant, and Residence, if out of the House in which the Death occurred.	When and where Registered, and Signature of Registrar.
58	Robert McCabe. Retired Ploughman. Married to Margaret Christie, Kirkliston	1899. September Thirtieth. 10h.0m.a.m. Broomhouse Kirkliston	M	68 Years	Robert McCabe Dealer in Vegetables (Dec). Margaret McCabe M.S. Hoggie (Dec)	Chronic Nephritis. 3 months. Cardiac failure. As cert by Alex. Kelso M.B. C.M. Broxburn	James McCabe Son (present)	1899. September 30th At Kirkliston Tho. Scott Registrar
59	John Hunter. Ploughman. Widower of Jane Reid, Kirkliston	1899. October Sixth. 3h.0m.a.m. Farm Cottages Riddry Kirkliston	M	90 Years	John Hunter Ploughman (Dec). Mary Hunter M.S. Napier (Dec)	Old age. As cert by A. Kelso M.B. C.M. Broxburn	John Hunter Son. Linlithgow Bridge	1899. October 6th At Kirkliston Tho. Scott Registrar
60	Alexander Bain Campbell. Coal miner. (Single)	1899. October Ninth. 3h.0m.a.m. Drumshoreland Hospital (Usual residence Boutris Bathgate)	M	17 Years	William Gatton Campbell Coal miner. Marion Campbell M.S. Fleming	Enteric fever 18 days. Perforation of Bowels. 3 hours. As cert by Alex. Stewart M.B. C.M. Uphall	William Gatton Campbell Father (Paulville Bathgate)	1899. October 9th At Kirkliston Tho. Scott Registrar

Tho. Scott Registrar.

Page of records for Kirkliston in West Lothian (Linlithgowshire) from the Statutory Register of Deaths.

- when and where the death was registered, and the signature of the registrar.

Between 1856 and 1860, the following information is also given:

- when the doctor last saw the deceased person (though, at this period, it's not uncommon to see an annotation of 'No medical attendant');

- the person's burial place, and the undertaker or other person by whom the burial was certified.

My 3x great-grandfather James Smith died in 1856. His death record shows he was buried in the churchyard of Belhelvie (a parish just north of Aberdeen), and that this was certified by the sexton, George Low.

As usual, the 1855 record gives much more information. As well as all the information in the 1856-60 death record, in 1855 there is also:

- the name of the deceased person's spouse;

- the forenames and ages of all their children, in order of birth.

In fact, although the heading of the relevant column in the death record from 1861 onwards simply asks 'whether single, married or widowed', it was the practice of the registrars to enter information about the deceased person's spouse. The name of a husband or late husband and his occupation would be entered, or a wife's or late wife's forename and maiden surname.

2 Census Records

INTRODUCTION

Taking a count of the population is not a new occurrence: 2,000 years ago a census of the Roman Empire took place or, as the Authorised Version of the Bible puts it, 'There went out a decree from Caesar Augustus that all the world should be taxed.' As well as the Romans, other ancient peoples (such as the Babylonians, Egyptians and Chinese) carried out numberings of their populations, mainly to find how much tax governments should be receiving, and how many men were liable to serve in their armies.

Today the emphasis is more on the allocation of government grants for education, employment, health, transport and racial inequality. According to the General Register Office for Scotland's website, central and local government, health authorities, businesses and community groups all benefit from the availability of accurate and reliable information from the census, and this should lead to better services for communities.

Modern censuses date from the 18th century, including the US Federal Census, which was first taken in 1790. The United Kingdom took its first census in 1801 in Scotland, England, Wales and the Channel Islands, and further censuses followed every ten years (apart from 1941, because of the disruption due to the Second World War). The first censuses in the Isle of Man and Ireland followed in 1811 and 1821 respectively. The names of individual people were not required until 1841, but in a very few areas quite detailed information was collected by those undertaking the census count locally, and some of this information has survived among parish records.

When the first official census of Scotland was taken in 1801, the country's population was found to be 1,608,420. A hundred years later, this had increased to 4,472,103. The population of Scotland in 2001 was 5,062,011, of whom 87.15 per cent were born in Scotland. In addition, 818,966 people born in Scotland were living in England and Wales in 2001. (In comparison, over the last two centuries, the population of England and Wales has risen from 8,892,536 to 52,041,916.)

At the beginning of 2004, images of the 1891 and 1901 census records for Scotland were available to download in digitised form from the *ScotlandsPeople* website (www. scotlandspeople.gov.uk). The 1881 census was also available there, but in transcript form, produced by the Church of Jesus Christ of Latter-day Saints (the 'Mormons') (see Chapter 9). Images of the records in the 1881 census were expected to become available online during 2004, as were those from the censuses taken in 1841, 1851, 1861 and 1871, with indexes similar to those for 1891 and 1901.

1891 AND 1901 CENSUSES

To find a record in either the 1891 or 1901 censuses, you need to call up the 'Search Census (1891, 1901)' screen. As with a search for a statutory birth, marriage or death record, all you *must* enter is a surname. Unless you're looking for an unusual name like 'Sirett', however, of which there is only one occurrence in the 1901 census, you would do well to enter a forename, county or enumeration district, and an age range.

When you click on the 'search' button, the screen refreshes with an extra line telling you how many entries have been found. If you've left both the '1891' and '1901' boxes ticked, the number of entries will be those found in both censuses. Clicking on either box will remove the tick, allowing you to search in just one census year.

To see the list of entries that match your search, click on the 'view' button, which will cost you one credit. To then see the actual census entry, click on the 'view' button against the appropriate line in the list, which will cost you a further five credits.

'Search 1891/1901 Census' page on ScotlandsPeople website.

A separate window will open, showing a page from the census enumerator's return for the particular area, with details of the person or family you're looking for.

The information in the census records is similar for 1891 and 1901. Both records list:

- the road or street, and the number or name of the house;
- the forename and surname of each person;
- his or her relationship to the head of the household;
- the marital status of each adult;
- each person's age at his or her last birthday (with males' and females' ages listed in separate columns);
- the occupation of each person;
- whether he or she was an employer, a worker or self-employed;
- each person's birthplace;
- whether he or she could speak Gaelic, or Gaelic and English;
- whether the person was deaf and dumb, blind, a 'lunatic', an imbecile, an idiot (in 1891) or feeble-minded (in 1901);
- how many rooms the dwelling contained that had one window or more.

The 1901 census asked, in addition, whether each person worked at home.

Of all the information contained in a census record, age is the least reliable. The older people became, the more years they would drop of their age. Until they reached their late eighties or nineties, that is, when they would proudly proclaim how old they were.

Even children's ages are often found to be incorrectly stated in census entries, although I should imagine that this happened as a result of parents' difficulties in keeping track of the ages of their (often large) families, rather than any deliberate attempt to deceive.

I have also noticed that the place of birth of an adult relative may well be incorrect in a census entry. The head of the household may have believed that his or her brother or sister had been born in the same place as the head, while that may not have been the case.

In the 1851 census, my 3x great-grandmother Joan Walker, as head of her household, stated wrongly that her unmarried sister Mary Brodie came from 'Roxburghshire, Galashiels', which was Joan's own birthplace. Twenty years later Mary's birthplace was given correctly as 'Peeblesshire, Innerleithen'. I wonder if this was because the new head of the household, Mary's nephew George Tait, didn't know where his aunt was from, and had to ask her.

Criteria : Censuses : 1901; Surname: "MCKENZIE"; Use Soundex; Forename: "DONALD"; County: Midlothian; Age From: 50; Age To: 70

No.	Year	Surname	Forename	Sex	Age	District	County	GROS Data	Image	Extract
1	1901	MACKENZIE	DONALD	M	54	CRAMOND	MIDLOTHIAN	679/00 001/000 021	View (5 credits)	Order
2	1901	MACKENZIE	DONALD	M	59	ST ANDREW EDIN	MIDLOTHIAN	685/02 086/000 021	View (5 credits)	Order
3	1901	MACKENZIE	DONALD	M	57	NEWINGTON	MIDLOTHIAN	685/05 078/000 014	View (5 credits)	Order
4	1901	MACKENZIE	DONALD	M	56	ST GEORGE	MIDLOTHIAN	685/01 061/000 015	View (5 credits)	Order
5	1901	MACKENZIE	DONALD	M	62	LEITH N	MIDLOTHIAN	692/01 027/A00 047	View (5 credits)	Order
6	1901	MACKEZIE	DONALD F	M	60	LIBERTON	MIDLOTHIAN	693/01 001/000 025	View (5 credits)	Order
7	1901	MCKECHNIE	DONALD	M	64	ST ANDREW EDIN	MIDLOTHIAN	685/02 092/000 001	View (5 credits)	Order
8	1901	MCKENZIE	DONALD	M	57	COLINTON	MIDLOTHIAN	677/00 006/000 018	View (5 credits)	Order
9	1901	MCKENZIE	DONALD	M	63	CANONGATE	MIDLOTHIAN	685/03 107/000 003	View (5 credits)	Order
10	1901	MCKENZIE	DONALD	M	55	ST GILES	MIDLOTHIAN	685/04 051/000 007	View (5 credits)	Order

List of the results returned by a search in the 1901 census.

Page from the 1901 census for Tingwall, Whiteness and Weisdale in Shetland.

Middle names aren't usually specified in census returns. If you're lucky, you'll find a middle initial or two, but this isn't always given. So, if you're looking for 'James Alfred Smith' and you find 'James Smith', this doesn't mean he isn't 'your' James.

With surnames, the problem is more often with the indexing, rather than the name being incorrect in the original census entry. Unfortunately, the original census books were written up by the enumerators by hand, and while many of the entries are perfectly clear, there are also others where the handwriting is very difficult to read. This has led, unsurprisingly, to names being wrongly indexed. Errors also occur in the indexing of ages, due to the enumerators' practice of scoring through the ages in performing the head count.

In addition, although the 'soundex' facility on the search pages is helpful, it will not always pick up all the variants of the surname you're looking for (and sometimes it'll list some you wouldn't expect). A little 'trial and error' goes a long way!

1881 CENSUS

The search for the 1881 census is different to that for 1891 and 1901, because the database index being searched was produced by the Church of Jesus Christ of Latter-day Saints. To find an entry in the index, you call up the 'Search Census (1881)' screen. For this census, the least information you can enter is either a surname or an address.

As with the other censuses, when you click on the 'search' button, the screen refreshes with an additional line stating the number of matching entries that have been found. To see the list of entries, you click on the 'view' button, which will cost you one credit.

At the beginning of 2004, you couldn't yet see an on-screen image of the page from the enumerator's return. Instead, at the cost of just one additional credit, you could see a transcript of the information for the relevant household. To print out the page, you could click on the 'print screen' button in the top left-hand corner of the screen.

The information available on the 1881 census is similar to that provided for the other two census years, but **without**:

- whether a person was an employer, a worker or self-employed;
- whether he or she could speak Gaelic, or Gaelic and English;

The actual images of the 1881 census records were expected to become available during 2004 on the *ScotlandsPeople* website, on the same basis as those for 1891 and 1901. The separate search screen was expected to be kept, however, as the 1881 index allowed more flexible searching than the indexes for the other years.

1851-1871 CENSUSES

The images and indexes for the Scottish censuses for 1841, 1851, 1861 and 1871 were also expected to become available on the *ScotlandsPeople* site during 2004. The search screens for the 1841-1871 censuses were expected to be similar to those for 1891 and 1901. The information in the census returns for 1851-1871 was fairly similar to that for 1891 and 1901, and listed:

- the road or street, and the number or name of the house;
- the forename and surname of each person;
- his or her relationship to the head of the household;
- the marital status of each adult;
- each person's age at his or her last birthday (with males' and females' ages listed in separate columns);
- the occupation of each person;
- his or her birthplace;
- whether the person was deaf and dumb, blind, a 'lunatic', an imbecile, or an idiot (in 1871);
- how many rooms the dwelling contained that had one window or more (from 1861);
- the number of children in each family (aged 5-15 in 1861, and 6-18 in 1871) attending school, or (in 1871) being educated at home.

1841 CENSUS

The 1841 census returns contain less information than the later records, this being:

- the road or street, and the number or name of the house;
- the forename and surname of each person;
- each person's age at his or her last birthday (with males' and females' ages listed in separate columns);
- the occupation of each person;
- whether he or she was born in the county or not.

You'll note that the exact county and parish of birth is not specified, nor is the relationship of the person to the head of the household – in fact, there is no head. A man and a woman living together who share the same surname may be married,

Page from the 1841 census for Farr in Sutherland.

but then again they may be brother and sister. In addition, in the 1841 records, ages above 15 are (supposed to be) rounded down to the nearest five (e.g. '24' would be stated as '20').

1801-1831 CENSUSES

Before 1841 the census enumerators were not required to compile detailed lists of those living in their districts, but some did anyway. Detailed lists of inhabitants still survive from these and other early censuses for a few parishes in 26 of the 33 historic counties of Scotland. You can find information about them in the booklets *Local Census Listings 1522-1930: Holdings in the British Isles* by Jeremy Gibson and Mervyn Medlycott and *Pre-1841 Censuses & Population Listings in the British Isles* by Colin R. Chapman (see Bibliography). These early censuses are not yet available online.

3 Old Parish Registers

INTRODUCTION

Before the introduction of civil registration in Scotland in 1855, baptisms, marriages or banns, and burials were recorded by the parish authorities of the Church of Scotland (it was usually the schoolteacher or session clerk who kept the register), irrespective of the creed of the people involved. No doubt there were members of other congregations – and perhaps Church of Scotland ministers too – who were none too happy with this situation, and the recording of many of these events increasingly slipped through the net as time went on. This was the case following the breakaway of various Presbyterian bodies through the 18th century, and, especially, with the formation of the Free Church of Scotland in 1843 (see Chapter 11).

There are a number of reasons why many events aren't recorded in the parish registers. One is that the dates from which different parishes began to keep registers varied quite widely. While the first instruction to do so (from a Council of pre-Reformation clergy) appeared in 1552, it wasn't until after 1560 that registers began to be kept in any widespread way, and many parishes' registers don't start (or survive from) earlier than the middle of the 16th century. Another reason that many events weren't recorded in the parish registers was the imposition in 1783 of a stamp duty of three old pence on every baptism, marriage and burial entry in the register. Refusal to pay the duty left people liable to a five pounds penalty. The GROS reports that whole parishes – and the entire county of Sutherland – were alleged to have stopped keeping parish registers altogether. The duty was repealed in 1794, but the effects may have been longer lasting.

Writing a few years before the introduction of civil registration in Scotland, George Seton pointed out that although the figures from the censuses of 1841 and 1851 showed Scotland's population to be rising, parish register entries indicated just the opposite. Seton's estimate of the number of births in Sutherland was 800 per year, whereas the actual number registered in 1842 was 470. By 1850 this had dropped to only 74.

As far as Scotland's three largest cities of the time were concerned, Seton estimated that the average annual population increases for Glasgow, Edinburgh and Dundee should have been around 10,000, 4,800 and 2,250 respectively. The actual numbers of baptisms recorded in the registers of the three cities were 2,646, 1,077 and 531, i.e. less than 25 per cent of Seton's estimates.

Even if his estimates were rather on the high side – Seton was making the case for changing over to civil registration – nevertheless, many events were simply not recorded. Don't despair, however, as over six million baptisms and three and a half million marriages *are* in the *ScotlandsPeople* (www.scotlandspeople.gov.uk) indexes.

Compared to England, Scotland has relatively few parishes: just over 900 in the whole country, whereas the English county of Norfolk alone has about 700. (See Appendix 2 for more information on the Scottish parishes.) Unlike England, Scotland has no bishops in its national church and, consequently, there are no Bishop's Transcripts of the parish registers.

Since 1855, however, Scotland *has* had the advantage over England, in that all of its parish registers (over 8,000) have been stored together in Edinburgh. Well, this was an advantage for those who lived in the capital city, or could get there easily. All the rest of us – whether we lived elsewhere in Scotland, on the other side of the world, or somewhere in between – have had to wait for the arrival of the Internet and the digitisation of the Old Parish Registers (OPRs) for this to become an advantage for us too. (To be fair, though, the Mormons and many libraries had microform copies of the registers and indexes.)

Although the earliest Scottish register contains entries back to 1553 (for baptisms and banns in the parish of Errol, Perthshire), most don't stretch so far back in time. Of the seven parishes on the Isle of Skye in Inverness-shire, for example, the oldest register is that of Portree, which begins as late as 1800.

Scotland's major cities cover much larger areas today than they did in the past, and they include, as well as their old medieval centres, a number of what were predominantly rural surrounding areas. Modern-day Edinburgh, for instance, includes the whole of the following parishes formerly in the county of Midlothian (or Edinburghshire):

- Edinburgh (parish no. 685);
- St Cuthbert's (685/2);
- Canongate (685/3);
- North Leith (692/1);
- South Leith (692/2);

- Cramond (679);
- Corstorphine (678);
- Colinton (or Hailes) (677);
- Liberton (693);
- Duddingston (684).

In addition, today's City of Edinburgh unitary authority includes most of these former West Lothian (or Linlithgowshire) parishes:

- Dalmeny (665);
- Kirkliston (687);
- Currie (682).

BAPTISMS

To find the record of a baptism, you have to call up the 'Search Old Parish Register (OPR) Births/Christenings' screen. As with the statutory birth record, you only *need* to enter the surname you're looking for. If you know the forename, year range and parish as well, however, your search is likely to be more successful if you enter those details as well.

Page from the Register of Baptisms for the parish of Rosemarkie in Ross and Cromarty.

Click on the 'search' button, and the search screen will refresh showing you how many matching entries have been found. To see the list of entries, click on 'view', which will cost you one credit. It's expected that, during 2004, the facility to view the actual record online will be introduced. Clicking on a 'view' button against the particular entry you're interested in, should cause a new window to open with the image of the page in the parish register which contains that entry. This will cost a further five credits.

Compared with the statutory records, the parish records contain less information. They will usually tell you, however:

- the name of the child;

- the names of both parents, including the mother's maiden name (although it's not at all uncommon, especially among earlier entries, for there to be no mother's name at all);

- the date of the child's baptism (and in some cases, the date of birth too);

- in urban areas, the father's occupation;

- where the parents lived (strictly speaking, what you get in rural parishes is a man's 'territorial designation' – i.e. being 'in' or 'of' somewhere – which was not necessarily the place where he was living, especially in the case of larger landholders and 'the gentry');

- In earlier records, whether the child was 'lawful' or illegitimate.

As there was no standard format for parish records, there's a fair amount of variation in what the records of individual parishes contain. For example, the register for the parish of Belhelvie in Aberdeenshire shows that on 19 April 1830:

> Said day James Smith, blacksmith in Menie, had a son born by his wife Ann Cruickshank and baptized on the 9th May called James.

This entry, from the parish register of Stow in Midlothian, gives similar information:

> Walker, George, carter, Stow and Joan Brodie his spouse had a daughter born 27 April 1812, and baptized a few days after, called Mary.

Here is another example from the records of the parish of Moulin, Perthshire for the year 1833:

> Born October 11, baptized do. 22, a son to John McKenzie and Christian Gow his wife in Straloch, named Donald.

For these baptisms, you're given most of the information you'd get in the case of a civil registration birth record except the all-important date and place of the parents' marriage. The Moulin example, however, doesn't specify the father's occupation.

In the following tabular entry from the parish of Dunnet in Caithness, you also discover the names of witnesses:

Date of birth	1820 October 18th
Date of baptism	1820 October 19th
Parents' names	Alexr. Stewart
	Anne Allan
Child's name	Alexander
Parents' residence	Westside of Dunnet
Witnesses of baptism	David Sutherland
	Joyce Mitchel

This 1796 baptism from the parish register of Innerleithen in Peeblesshire also tells you the occupations of the witnesses:

> Mary, procreate betwixt James Brodie ploughman in Hilhouses and Mary Blake his spouse, was born upon the second day of April and baptized upon the twelfth day of the said month by the Revd. Mr. Robert Scott Minr. Of Innerleithen: Mr. Charles Brodie overseer of the manufactory and Robert Nicol servant to the said James Brodie witnesses.

BANNS AND MARRIAGES

You need to call up the 'Search Old Parish Register (OPR) Marriages/Banns' screen to search for those records. Enter at least the surname of one of the marriage partners, but preferably also the surname of the spouse, and any other information you have, and click on the 'search' button.

The page will refresh, showing in an extra line the number of entries found. If you click on the 'view' button, it will cost you one credit to see the list of matching entries. As with the birth entries, it should become possible during 2004 to view the actual marriage/banns record online. You should be able to click on 'view' on the line for the entry you believe to be the one you're searching for, and a new page should open showing the image of the record. This is expected to cost you five credits.

'Search Old Parish Register Marriages/Banns' page on ScotlandsPeople website.

List of the results of a search in the Old Parish Register banns and marriages.

Many of the earlier marriage entries in parish registers are rather bald and not very informative, such as this one from Traquair in Peeblesshire:

1788 Nov. 22 Charles Brodie and Nelly Henderson at Riggs married.

You'd have to look elsewhere to find who the couple's parents were or the occupation of Charles. This entry from the Edinburgh parish register for 12 November 1813 is more helpful:

Alexr. Steuart, soldier, 9th R.V.B., Edinb. Castle, and Ann Allan, Old Church Parish, daughter of the late Alexr. Allan, Caithness.

'R.V.B.' stands for Royal Veterans Battalion, which helped me to locate the discharge papers of my 3x great-grandfather Alexander Stewart via the [UK] National Archives' PROCAT online catalogue (see Chapter 6). Alexander's discharge certificate lists his 16 years of army service, as well as his place of birth, age at enlistment and previous occupation.

Many of the entries in the parish registers have primarily to do with recording the proclamation of banns leading to marriage, rather than recording the actual marriage itself. In the following case from the parish of Stow, Midlothian, the date of the actual marriage isn't specified. This entry does give the names of cautioners,

Marriages. Anno 1783 continued   2.

July 6th

John Watt Porter in Aberdeen & Anne Davidson in this parish signified their purpose of marriage by James Keith Elder & consigned pledges. Whereupon being orderly proclaimed they were married upon the twenty third day of July by Mr James Gregory

Watt & Davidson

12th

Alexander Connan Taylor & Katharine Lovie both in this parish signified their purpose of marriage & consigned pledges. Whereupon being orderly proclaimed they were married upon the second day of August by Mr John Skinner

Connan & Lovie

27th

Robert Ley in the parish of Coul & Margaret Ross in this parish of Old Machar signified their purpose of marriage by John Christie Elder who is cautioner for their pledges. Whereupon being orderly proclaimed they were married

Ley & Ross

August 3

William Ross and Mary Still both in this parish signified their purpose of marriage by George Stephen Elder who is cautioner for their pledges Whereupon being orderly proclaimed they were married

Ross & Still

9th

John Cooper mariner and Jean Bothwell both in Old Aberdeen signified their purpose of marriage John Bothwell being cautioner for their pledges. Whereupon being three several times proclaimed they were married upon the twenty third day of August by Mr Robert Dunbar

Cooper & Bothwell

Page of marriages from the Old Parish Register for the parish of Old Machar in Aberdeenshire.

who would have put up a 'caution': a sum of money in surety that the couple would actually marry:

> Tait, George, servant in Craigend and Margaret Walker, daughter of George Walker in Killochyett, gave in their names to be proclaimed in order to marry 14 January 1837. Cautioners Thomas Fin in Craigend and Robert Walker Killochyett. After due proclamation they were married.

Compare the following two entries in the parish register of Moulin, Perthshire for 1775 and 1777 respectively:

> Dec. 2nd John Stewart and Janet Forbes both in this parish were booked in order to be proclaimed for marriage.

> Novr. 29th John Stewart in this parish of Moulin and Janet Robertson in parish of Logierait were booked in order to be proclaimed for marriage and were married Decr. 11th.

The first entry doesn't mention whether the marriage actually took place. Do both entries refer to the same John Stewart? Did he fall out with his first fiancée and end up marrying a different Janet? You'd have to look for children born to both couples for the answer.

BURIALS

In comparison with the very helpful amount of information given in the statutory death records, burial entries in parish registers can be very brief, such as the following 1834 entry from the parish of Innerleithen in Peeblesshire:

> Nov. 16 This day Charles Brodie late of Lee was interred.

In the case of the burial of a child, the father's name is usually given, as in this extract from the register for 1833 for the neighbouring parish of Traquair, also in Peeblesshire:

> March 4 Charles son to Charles Brodie Innerleithen.

In many cases, rather than recording a burial as such, the entries actually record the hire of the parish mortcloth, which covered the coffin at the funeral, and will be in the form of an accounting entry.

During 2004 online viewing of burials in the OPRs should become available, although the GROS expects that there won't be an online index for these records for some time. Access to the OPR burials is therefore expected to be through some kind of browsing arrangement, allowing you to drill down through county to parish and then volume level.

Register of Deaths & Burials &c in the
Parish of Bourtie
1852

On the 22d day of March 1852, Widow MacLaw
in Old Meldrum & formerly residing at Loanside in this
Parish died, & was buried in the Church yard here
on the 24th Inst.

On the 26th April 1852, George Will aged 11 years
Son of Charles Will in this Parish died & was buried
here on the 28th Inst

On the 1st day of June 1852, George Thomas Bisset
aged ten years, Second Son, of the Revd Dr Bisset,
Minister of this Parish died, & was buried here on
the 5th Curt

On the 13th day of July 1852, Charlotte Knight
aged 18 years, Daughter of Benjamin Knight
in Old Meldrum died of Consumption & was buried
here on the 15th Curt

On the 13th day of July 1852, James Bisset
aged 23 years, Son of John Bisset in the Parish
of Methlic & lately in this Parish died of Consumption & was interred here on the 17th Curt

On the 8th day of August 1852, Mary Anderson
aged 8 years, daughter of John Anderson in Old Bourtie
died of Croup & was buried here on the 11th Curt

On the 29th day of September 1852, John Innes aged
13 years, Second Son of Peter Innes, Keith Hall was
interred here.

On the 8th day of October 1852, David Low, in Keith
Hall aged 73 years, died & was buried here on the 13th Curt

On the 24th day of October 1852, Sarah Jane Anderson,
Old Bourtie aged 11 months died of Croup & was buried
here on the 27th Curt

On the 29th Octr 1852, Alexr Duguid A Mill of Colly
hill had a Stillborn Daughter by his wife interred
here Same day

Page from the Register of Deaths and Burials for the parish of Bourtie in Aberdeenshire.

MONUMENTAL INSCRIPTIONS

Monumental inscriptions can often be more useful than burial records, as they usually indicate the age of the deceased person. On a gravestone there isn't much room for a great deal of information, but plaques on a church wall can be more informative. I was extremely lucky to discover this one in Traquair churchyard, on the outside wall of the church. The amount of detail given on the plaque spurred me on to carry out a lot of research:

In Memory
of
ALEXANDER BRODIE ESQ
Iron Master
late of Carey Street
in the Liberty of the Rolls London
and Calcut in the County of Salop
a Native of Traquaire
First inventor of
The Register Stoves and Fire Hearths for Ships
Had the honour of supplying
the whole BRITISH NAVY with the latter
for upwards of thirty years
To the preservation of many valuable lives
since their introduction
and was a great saving to Government
Died 6th January 1811
Aged 78 years
His mortal remains were deposited in
Chiswick Churchyard in the County of Middlesex
and
This tablet placed here by his
NEPHEWS AND NIECES
August 1818

It turned out that Alexander Brodie was my 6x great-uncle. He started out his career apprenticed to his father, Charles Brodie, who was the village blacksmith in Traquair. In 1751, when he was 18, Alexander set off for England, with 17 shillings and sixpence in his pocket and a letter of introduction from the mother-in-law of Lady Traquair. He made his fortune south of the Border, buying the Calcutts Ironworks near Ironbridge in Shropshire in 1786, and setting up a woollen factory in Innerleithen, Peeblesshire in the same year.

The GENUKI website (www.genuki.org.uk) (see Chapter 9) contains information on monumental inscriptions on its pages about individual parishes. In addition, many of the Scottish family history societies (see Chapter 14 and Appendix 5) have published transcriptions of the genealogical information to be found in the churches and churchyards in their areas. The transcriptions are available either in booklet form, on microfiche, or on CD-ROMs.

4 Wills and Inventories

INTRODUCTION

As well as using information from civil registration, parish records and the various censuses to locate your Scottish ancestors, you would be well advised to take a look at the index of Scottish wills and inventories at the *Scottish Documents* website (www.scottishdocuments.com). Digitised images of the documents, which span the period 1500 to 1901, can be downloaded from the site.

Now you may think that, although everyone high and low appeared (or at any rate should have appeared) in the parish registers, statutory records, and in the census, no-one in your family had enough money for him or her to bother making a will. Although it is certainly the case that most of the wills and inventories in the index were made by the upper classes and 'the gentry', this doesn't mean that no-one lower down the 'social scale' in past centuries ever had anything to leave. In the Glasgow Commissary Court alone, 80 labourers (many of them 'land labourers') or their widows are listed in the index between 1678 and 1823.

The *Scottish Documents* site contains images of the handwritten 'testaments' recorded by the clerks of the courts (originally the Commissary Courts, whose functions were taken over in the first quarter of the 19th century by the Sheriff Courts). These testaments were either 'testaments dative', where the deceased died intestate (i.e. had made no will), or 'testaments testamentar', where he or she had made a will. The purpose of the testament was to confirm executors for the estate of the deceased person.

In the case of a testament testamentar, the deceased person would have previously made a will (strictly speaking, a 'testamentary writing', as 'will' is not really Scottish legal terminology) such as a 'deed of settlement', in which executors were named. In the absence of such a document, the court would appoint an executor, often a creditor of the deceased. For both kinds of testament, an inventory would be drawn up, being an itemised list of the deceased's 'moveable' possessions (i.e. everything but land and buildings).

Land and buildings were 'heritable' property, which began to be included in testaments in the early 1800s. Previously it had been inherited by the eldest son according to the Scottish rules of succession. After the Heritable Jurisdictions Act

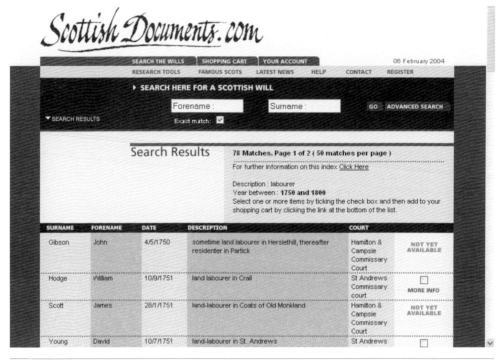

Results of a search in the Scottish Documents wills and inventories database.

had been passed in 1868, heritable land and buildings were regularly included in wills and inventories.

Commissary courts dealt with inheritance, and testaments in particular, and took over these functions from the earlier church courts. The first commissary court was set up in Edinburgh in 1564. A commissary was originally a bishop's official, but after the reformation of the Scottish church, he became an official of the court of the same name. The area under the jurisdiction of the commissary court was called the commissariot, whose boundaries corresponded to those of the medieval Scottish dioceses. From 1 January 1824, responsibility for confirming testaments passed to the existing sheriff courts, although some commissary courts continued in existence for a further 12 years.

The *Scottish Documents* index is a fully-searchable database of over 520,000 testaments, and can be searched free of charge, although there *is* a charge for downloading an actual testament (see Appendix 1). You can search by entering:

- the surname of the deceased person;
- his or her forename;
- the title, occupation or place of residence (where these are given) of the deceased;
- the court or commissariot in which the testament was recorded.

You can also specify start and end years for the search, and whether you want the resulting list of matching entries to be sorted (which can be by forename, surname or year). If the surname of the person you're looking for is very common in Scotland, you'll probably want to specify their forename too.

Although entering the deceased person's occupation or place of residence can help you to find relevant entries in the database, if that information is not contained in the index entry, specifying it in your search will make it harder to find entries. Beware of selecting a particular court, as sometimes testaments were recorded in the Edinburgh courts, which had jurisdiction over the whole of Scotland and Scots residing outside Scotland (as did the Prerogative Court of Canterbury for England).

The results list is in tabular form, and shows:

- surname;

- forename;

- date;

- description;

- court.

TESTAMENT DATIVE

There follows an example of a testament dative from 1871, complete with inventory, which relates to the estate of my 'reputed' great-great-grandfather Thomas Ritchie (*National Archives of Scotland, Alloa Sheriff Court registers of testaments, SC64/42/14*). Some of the language used in a testament such as this will be unfamiliar, either because the words are archaic, or legal jargon, or both! Fortunately, they're explained on the *Scottish Documents* website, and in even more detail on the Scottish Archive Network (SCAN) site (www.scan.org.uk). I've indicated some of those special words in bold in the testament dative.

A testament dative consists of three parts, the first of which is the introductory clause:

> At Alloa the eighth day of August eighteen hundred and seventy one
>
> In presence of George Monro Esquire, Commissary of the County of Clackmannan, **compeared** James Wallace, Solicitor, Alloa, as **Procurator** for the person after named and designed, and gave in the Inventory of the Personal Estate of Thomas Ritchie, Woodmerchant and Innkeeper at Forestmill, in the Parish and County of Clackman-nan, and affidavit thereto, after inserted, desiring that the same might be recorded in the Commissary Court Books of said Commissariot, which desire the said Commissary found reasonable, and ordained the same to be done accordingly, whereof the tenor follows Vizt.:

'Compear' means 'present oneself or appear, usually before a court', and a 'procurator' is a person (usually a solicitor) authorised to act on behalf of someone else. The second clause deals with the inventory:

> Inventory of the Personal Estate & Effects, wheresoever situated, of the late Thomas Ritchie, Woodmerchant and Innkeeper at Forestmill, in the Parish & County of Clackmannan, who died there on or about the twentieth day of June last, Eighteen hundred and Seventy one, made and given up by Andrew McQueen, Corn Merchant in Alloa, **Executor dative** qua Creditor **decerned** to the deceased by the Commissary of the County of Clackmannan, on the twenty first day of July, Eighteen hundred and Seventy one years.
>
> | | £ | s. | d. |
> |---|---|---|---|
> | I. Household Furniture, Goods, Stock in trade, Horses, Engine and Appurtenances and other effects belonging to the deceased, conform to Inventory and Valuation thereof by Alexander Thomson, Licensed Appraiser, Alloa, dated 2nd August 1871 | 72 | 19 | 2 |
> | II. Poultry within premises occupied by deceased at Forestmill | 0 | 11 | 0 |
> | III. Proportion from 15th May last to 20th June 1871 (being date of deceased's death) of Annuity of £100 contained in and due by Bond of Annuity by the English & Scottish Law Life Assurance Association in favor of George Cunningham, Civil Engineer, Edinburgh, and Alexander Moncrieff, Writer to the Signet, Perth, as Trustees of the late David Ritchie, for behoof of the deceased, dated 28 August 1866 | 9 | 17 | 3 |
> | | 84 | 7 | 5 |
>
> (sig.) Andrew McQueen, John Ewing Comy. Clk.

'Decerned' means 'pronounced judicially'. An 'executor dative' is one appointed by the court, rather than nominated in the deceased person's will, so 'executor dative qua creditor' means someone to whom the deceased owed money and who has formally been pronounced to be the executor of the deceased's estate by the court.

The third part of a testament dative is the confirmation clause:

> At Alloa, the eighth day of August one thousand eight hundred and Seventy one years
>
> In presence of John Ewing Esquire, Commissary Clerk of the County of Clackmannan, appeared Andrew McQueen, Corn Merchant in Alloa, **Executor dative** qua Creditor of the deceased Thomas Ritchie, Woodmerchant and Innkeeper at Forestmill, in the Parish and County of Clackmannan, who being solemnly sworn and examined **deponed**:
>
> That the said Thomas Ritchie died at Forestmill upon or about the twentieth day of June last, Eighteen hundred and Seventy one, and the **deponent** is about to enter upon the possession and management of the deceased's Personal Estate as **Executor dative** qua Creditor **decerned** to him by the Commissary of the County of Clackmannan, conform to Decree dative in his favor dated twenty first July Eighteen hundred and Seventy one.

That the **Deponent** does not know of any Testamentary Settlement or other Writing left by the deceased relative to the disposal of his personal estate and effects, or any part thereof.

That the foregoing Inventory which is signed by the said **deponent** and the said Commissary Clerk as relative hereto, is a full and complete Inventory of the Personal Estate and Effects of the said deceased Thomas Ritchie, wheresoever situated, and belonging or due to him beneficial at the time of his death, including the proceeds which have accrued thereon down to this date, in so far as the same has come to the **Deponent's** knowledge.

That the **Deponent** does not know of any money or property belonging to the deceased liable to the duty imposed by the Acts Twenty third Victoria, Chapter Fifteen, and Twenty third & Twenty fourth Victoria, Chapter Eighty.

Neither does he know of any money belonging to the deceased secured on heritage or heritable Bonds liable in duty.

That the value at this date of the said Personal Estate & Effects situated in the United Kingdom including the proceeds accrued thereon down to this date is under one hundred pounds Sterling.

That confirmation of said Personal Estate is required in favor of the **Deponent**.

All which is truth as the **deponent** shall answer to God.

(Sig.) Andw. McQueen, John Ewing Comy. Clk.

A 'deponent' is 'someone who makes a deposition before a court', while a 'deposition' is 'the testimony of a witness put down in writing'. So when we read that someone 'deponed', we can take that as 'made a written statement'.

TESTAMENT TESTAMENTAR

A testament testamentar consists of four parts: the three parts that appear in a testament dative as described above, plus the deceased person's will, which comes between the inventory and the confirmation clauses. As an example, here is a 'Deed of Settlement' made by my 4x great-grandfather James Brodie in 1825, taken from a testament testamentar *(National Archives of Scotland, Peebles Sheriff Court registers of testaments, SC42/20/3)*:

> Know all men by these presents, I James Brodie, feuar in Innerleithen, considering that it is my duty to settle my affairs in my lifetime, so as to prevent any disputes which might arise after my death **anent** the succession and division of my means and effects, and for other good reasons and causes, have resolved to make the settlement under written;

'Anent' is an old Scots word meaning 'concerning'.

> And therefore, and in consideration of the confidence which I repose in the persons after named, I do hereby assign, **dispone**, convey and make over to and in favor of John Brodie residing in Northgate of Peebles, my cousin, and Alexander Murray Bartram of **Templebar** Esquire, or to such of them as may accept, and to the survivor or acceptor & their assignees, as trustees and executors for the uses, ends and pur-

poses after mentioned, all and whole, my heritable property wherever situated, and of whatever description, with the exceptions after mentioned;

'Dispone' is more or less the same as 'convey and make over'. 'Templebar' is near Peebles, not the place of the same name in London.

As also all and sundry debts whether heritable or moveable, sums of money, principal and interest, penalty and expences, now resting and owing to me, & which shall be resting to me at the time of my decease, or may fall due thereafter by any person or persons whomsoever, or other ways, with all bonds heritable and moveable, bills, **decreets**, accounts, or any other way, and all grounds, vouchers, or instructions, or other writts or evidents whatsoever, lying money, gold and silver, coined or uncoined, bank bills, notes, or receipts, household furniture, and all other moveable **goods and gear** whatsoever, now pertaining and belonging to me, or which shall happen to pertain to me at the time of my decease, and which shall fall, accrue, belong and pertain to me afterwards, in and through the death of **the late Mr. Alexander Brodie of Carrey Street London, my uncle**, or any other manner of way whatever;

'Decreets' are 'awards by a court', while 'goods and gear' (or in Scots: 'guids and geir') are moveable rather than heritable possessions. The mention of Alexander Brodie was very helpful to me, as it confirmed my suspicion that my ancestor James Brodie was indeed a nephew of the 18th-century iron master (see Chapter 3).

Dispensing with the generality hereof, and admitting the same to be as valid and effectual to all intents and purposes, as if every species of my means and subjects heritable and moveable, goods and gear, were herein particularly inserted surrogating and substituting my said trustees and executors before named, or survivor accepting in my full right and place of the premises forever;

With full power to them or him immediately after my death, to enter into immediate possession of the whole property, means, and effects, as well as those belonging to me at the time, as those that may thereafter fall due, accrue pertain and belong to me from the residue of my said uncle's means and estate, or other ways.

And with power also to uplift, receive the same, and **intromit** therewith, all hereby **disponed**, conveyed and made over to my said trustees and executors, or survivor, pursue therefor, **compone**, transact and agree concerning the same, and to grant receipts and discharges thereof,

'Intromit' means 'take up the possession and management of property belonging to someone else', and 'compone' is 'make a payment to a feudal superior on the succession of an heir to land'.

And to sell and dispose of the same, heritable and moveable of every description, with the exception of the heritable subjects herein after mentioned, and that either publicly or privately, and at such times and places as they or he may think fit, and generally to do, and exerce all and every thing **thereanent**, that I might have done myself, before granting hereof,

And with power also to my said trustees and executors, or survivor of them to grant all necessary deeds, or powers, for the receipt and recovery of any sum or sums, share or shares of money, which may fall due to me, or my heirs or executors, after my death, from the Court of Chancery, or otherways,

And to grant all requisite powers of attorney, acquittances, and discharges, thereof, and therefor, the same as I could have done myself, but which whole subjects disponed and assigned, are conveyed by me in trust always for the uses, ends, and purposes, and under the conditions, reservations, and limitations after mentioned vizt.

In the first place, my said trustees and executors, or the survivor of them, as aforesaid, shall satisfy and pay all my just and lawful debts, that shall be resting and owing by me at the time of my death, with the expence of my funeral, which I recommend to them, to be respectable, although not extravagant; and the expence of executing this trust.

And in the second place, my said trustees and executors, or survivor of them as aforesaid shall make payment to my children of the sums of money and others underwritten vizt.

To pay to **Johan Brodie, my daughter, wife of George Walker at Killochyate near Stow**, the sum of ten pounds sterling, over and above three hundred pounds sterling, and upwards, already paid by me to, and for her, and her husband, payable at the first term of Whitsunday or Martinmas after my death, and I will and appoint that the sum of thirty pounds sterling be paid to her children, share and share alike, at the first term of Whitsunday or Martinmas that shall first happen after the marriage of either, or arriving at the age of twenty one, severally, and these provisions over and above the fee of said subjects at Killochyate which I have by the deeds thereof provided to them, after my own death,

The mention of a bequest to Joan (or 'Johan' as it says here) Brodie, who was my 3x great-grandmother and had married George Walker in Edinburgh in 1811, proved that this James Brodie was my ancestor.

Third, to pay to or for, Mary Brodie my second daughter **by the first marriage** an yearly annuity of thirteen pounds sterling during her lifetime, to commence from the the first term of Whitsunday or Martinmas after my death, and half yearly at these terms thereafter,

Fourth, to pay to each of **Margaret and Elizabeth Brodie**, my daughters the sum of three hundred pounds sterling, and that upon their attaining, severally, the age of twenty one years, or their marriage, the interest thereof, or such part of the same, to go to, and be applied in payment, of board, education, and cloathing as my trustees and executors may judge proper,

Fifth, to pay to **James Brodie my youngest son**, the sum of six hundred pounds sterling, at the age, or event, last before mentioned, and the interest of the same, to be applied as aforesaid,

Declaring always, that my said trustees and executors, or survivor, shall have power to call for sufficient security, from the before named legatees, and that before payment to them, for payment of the before mentioned annuity, and conform, and in proportion to the sums, they may respectively receive,

And sixth, I hereby will and declare, that after payment and fulfilment of the foresaid sums, debts, and provisions, herein before specified, and expence of, and attending this trust, the whole residue and remainder of my means and estate belonging to me at my death, with the exception of the heritable subject after mentioned, disponed to my youngest son James Brodie, on which may fall, accrue, and belong to me thereafter, shall belong exclusively to **Alexander Brodie my eldest son**, and that, upon his attaining the age of twenty five years compleat,

My said trustees or executors, or survivor, however retaining always, wherewith to pay and satisfy the before mentioned legacies, and annuity, with the assistance of the others as before specified, recommending to, and appointing that my said executors and trustees, shall have my said sons Alexander and James Brodie suitably kept, and educated, out of the means hereby provided to them, and settled in a business or profession according to their wish and station in the world,

I'd found through my researches that the parents of Joan Brodie (baptised in 1792 in Galashiels, Selkirkshire) and Mary Brodie (in 1796 in Innerleithen) were James Brodie and Mary Blake, who had married in 1789 in Selkirk. I'd also come across the marriage of a James Brodie and Agnes Walker in Innerleithen in 1811, but I didn't know whether this was the same James Brodie or a different one. The children of this marriage had been Margaret, Alexander, Elizabeth and James, all baptised in Innerleithen in 1812, 1813, 1815 and 1817 respectively. This will proved that it was the same James Brodie who had married again. The children of this second marriage were aged between eight and thirteen when James made his will (he died less than two months afterwards).

Declaring that in the event of the death of the said Alexander Brodie, my eldest son, before the age of twenty five, and his not having lawful children of his own body; and in the event of my said son James Brodie surviving him, then the residue or remainder which would have belonged to said Alexander Brodie, or his lawful children shall fall, accrue, and belong to said James Brodie, and his lawful children,

And in case of the deaths, of said Alexander Brodie and said James Brodie, and no lawful children of their bodies, then I will appoint and ordain, that my said trustees or executors, or survivor of them, pay what sum or share which would have fallen to them, as said residue or reversion, to the children or child of my last marriage, who may survive their said brothers, share and share alike;

And failing either of my said daughters, Margaret and Elizabeth Brodie by death, and leaving lawful issue, the child or children of the deceased shall have the share that would have belonged to their deceased parent,

These preceding paragraphs of the will make it very clear what should happen in the event of the death of any of the children of James's second marriage.

And I do hereby, and besides the foresaid sum of six hundred pounds sterling, dispone, assign, convey, and make over to and in favour of my said son James Brodie, his heirs and assignees that piece of ground, lately leased or fued by me, from the Right Honourable Charles, Earl of Traquaire near the road leading to the mineral well of Innerleithen, and upon part of which I have since built a dwelling house, together with the said building itself and lease or feu contract by which I hold the same,

And I do farther, and over and above the foresaid residue and reversion of my means and effects as before mentioned, dispone, assign, convey, and make over to and in favour of my eldest son Alexander Brodie, his heirs and assignees the ground and houses in the village of Innerleithen possessed by myself, and sometime ago purchased by me from Helen Henderson, alias Brodie, residing in Innerleithen, together with the title deeds by which I hold the same;

And I declare that the provisions hereby made to my children, before written, with what the said Johan Brodie, my daughter, and her husband have already received, or what has been advanced to and for them, together with the same liferent and fee of the foresaid subjects at Killochyate, is in full of all **legittim bairns' part of gear**, or other claims whatever, which might be competual to them, in and through my decease, any manner of way,

Under Scottish law, the children of a deceased person were entitled to a third of his estate if their mother was still alive, or a half if she was already dead. This was the 'legitim' or 'bairns' part'. The father could choose how to dispose of only a third (or a half) of his estate under the terms of his will, and this was known as the 'dead's part'.

And in case any of them shall not be satisfied with the terms hereof, and shall make any claim, directly or indirectly, for a larger share of my means and estate, or shall attempt to quarrel, or reduce this present settlement on these or any other grounds whatever, I hereby declare that he, she, or they shall forfeit and lose all right they have in the premises in consequence hereof, and their share portion or provision shall belong equally to those who may be satisfied herewith;

I have the feeling that the provisions of the previous paragraph would be considered unfair nowadays!

And farther, as an inducement for my said trustees and executors to accept of the office and trust hereby committed to them, I declare that they shall not be liable for neglect, ommissions, nor diligence of any kind, nor shall be liable *singuli in solidum*, but each only for his own personal intromissions. And they shall be no farther liable for any factor or agent they may appoint (which they are hereby authorised to do) than that they shall be habit and repute responsible at the time of entering upon the office;

And for carrying these presents more effectually into execution, I hereby nominate and appoint my said trustees, or survivor accepting for the uses, ends, and purposes foresaid, to be my sole and only executors and intromitters, with my goods and gear of every description, with power to them or him to give up inventories of my effects and to confirm if needful;

And I exclude and debar all others from the office, and farther I hereby nominate and appoint them or the survivor to be tutors and curators, or sole tutor and curator, to my children under age with all powers and faculties competent to such reserving always my own liferent of the premises;

With full power at any time in my life, and even upon death bed, by a writing under my hand to alter, innovate, or revoke these presents, in whole or in part, and to assign or dispose of the effects hereby conveyed, as I may think proper,

But in so far as these presents shall not be altered, the same shall be valid and sufficient, and effectual, although found lying by me, at the time of my death, or in the custody of any other person undelivered, and with the delivery hereof, I hereby dispense;

And I do farther revoke, rescind, and recall, and declare of no avail force or effect, any Deed or Deeds of Settlement I may formerly have made and executed;

And I consent to the registration hereof in the Books of Council & Session, or other books competent, therein to remain for preservation, and for that purpose constitute the said Thomas Thomson Esquire Advocate my procurators, etc.

In witness whereof I have subscribed these presents, written upon this and the five preceding pages of stamped paper, by James Bartram Writer in Peebles,

At Innerleithen the second day of May one thousand eight hundred and twenty five years,

Before these witnesses: the said James Bartram and John Fothringham Writer in Edinburgh,

(signed) James Brodie, J Bartram witness, John Fothringham witness

Part Two

Other Information and Indexes Available Online

5 Emigration and Immigration Databases

INTRODUCTION

According to a report commissioned in 2003 by the Ancestral Tourism Industry Steering Group, around 50 million people of Scots descent are scattered in many countries around the world, mainly in the United States, Canada, Australia and New Zealand. For those of you reading this book in the United States, Canada or Australia, extra online help is available in the form of databases containing records of some of the immigrants to your countries.

The American Family Immigration History Center's database of immigrants arriving in the US through Ellis Island in New York Harbour covers the period 1892-1924, while the National Archives of Canada's ArchiviaNet has a database of immigrants to Canada between 1925 and 1935. The indexes of the immigrants to the Australian states of New South Wales and Victoria cover the periods 1839-1896 and 1839-1911 respectively, while the Highlands and Islands Emigration Society database covers emigration from Scotland to Australia between 1852 and 1857.

HIGHLANDS AND ISLANDS EMIGRATION SOCIETY DATABASE

The Highlands and Islands Emigration Society was founded through private sub-scription to enable people who were destitute to emigrate to Australia. The National Archives of Scotland (NAS, formerly the Scottish Record Office) holds passenger lists for 1852-1857, during which period the society arranged the emigration of 5,000 Highlanders and Islanders.

The passenger list can be searched online by forename and/or surname at www. scan.org.uk/researchtools/emigration.htm. The results page shows the emigrant's:

- family number;
- surname;
- forenames;
- age;
- birthyear*;
- place of residence;
- estate (e.g. Lord Macdonald's);
- parish*;
- county*;
- ship;
- date of departure;
- port of departure;
- port of arrival;
- remarks.

Clicking on the family number brings up a screen showing the whole family. The fields marked with an asterisk have been inserted into the record by SCAN staff. The birthyear has been calculated by simply subtracting the person's age from the year in the date of departure. The parish and county have been added to show where the place of residence was located.

US IMMIGRATION: ELLIS ISLAND

Ellis Island lies in New York harbour, about halfway between Liberty Island, home of the Statue of Liberty, and the large island of Manhattan. Between 1892 and 1954 over 12 million immigrants to the United States entered the country via the reception centre on Ellis Island, with an average of 5,000 processed per day. The centre became less important after the First World War, however, and finally closed in 1954.

Thirty years later, the main building was restored in a $162 million project, culminating in the opening in 1990 of the Ellis Island Immigration Museum. Visitors to the museum can see exhibits on the history of immigration and ethnicity in the US, find out how immigrants were processed through the centre, see cherished items brought from their homelands, and learn about the peak immigration years 1880-1924.

According to the museum's website (www.ellisisland.com), over 100 million of today's Americans (i.e. over a third) are descended from immigrants who passed through the Ellis Island centre. Over 5 million people from Britain have emigrated to the United States, 2.3 million of these in the peak period.

AMERICAN FAMILY IMMIGRATION HISTORY CENTER DATABASE

Through the website www.ellisisland.org, the American Family Immigration History Center (AFIHC) provides an online database of information on ships' passengers and crew members. To find an immigrant, you enter his or her surname and, optionally, forename in the search boxes and click on the 'search' button, which brings up a list of immigrants with that name.

Click on one of these names, and a 'Passenger Record' screen will be displayed, listing the person's:

- name;
- ethnicity;
- place of residence in the United States (if applicable);
- date of arrival;
- age on arrival;

- gender;
- marital status;
- ship sailed on;
- port of departure;
- and whether he or she was a US citizen.

If you click on the button marked 'View original ship manifest', a page will display showing an image of the original list of passengers, and indicating on which line of the document your ancestor is listed. You can buy a copy of the ship's manifest through the AFIHC website, if you wish. You can also display the manifest on your computer in text form, which can be easier to read, but isn't quite the same as seeing the original.

By clicking on the 'View ship' button, you can then see a photograph of the ship on which your ancestor or relative sailed to the United States, together with some information about it. You can also buy a copy of this photograph through the website.

If you join the Statue of Liberty-Ellis Island Foundation (SOLEIF), which raises funds for the restoration and preservation of the Statue of Liberty and Ellis Island, you'll have access to additional facilities on the AFIHC website, where you can:

- annotate passenger records with notes (which can be read by all visitors to the site);

- create a Family History Scrapbook, with a free print or CD-ROM copy.

You can create the first 16 pages of your Family History Scrapbook free of charge. The scrapbook can contain photographs and sound recordings as well as text, and can either be kept private or added to the website's Family History Archive.

CANADIAN IMMIGRATION: PIER 21

Pier 21 in Halifax is Canada's equivalent of Ellis Island, and was the country's main immigration port from 1928-1971. Scots have been emigrating to Canada for 400 years – the first Canadian Prime Minister, Sir John Macdonald, was a Scot – and appropriately enough, Halifax is the capital of Nova Scotia (New Scotland).

The Pier 21 website (www.pier21.ca) describes how the building was refurbished and opened as a museum in 1999. At the site, you can buy an image of the ship your ancestor sailed to Canada on. The site also holds a number of fascinating, and sometimes harrowing, accounts of some of the people who passed through Pier 21. These include displaced persons and refugees, evacuee children, 'home children', immigrants, servicemen (who left from Pier 21 to fight in the Second World War), and war brides, as well as staff and volunteers who worked at Pier 21.

Many of the Scots immigrants to Canada willingly chose a new life there for themselves and their families, but some were forced to go as a result of the 'Highland Clearances'. This was a shameful period when Scottish landlords removed their tenants to make room for more profitable sheep and deer.

At the website of the National Archives of Canada (www.archives.ca), you can use the ArchiviaNet online research tool to search a number of databases, including those for immigration records (1925-1935) and 'home children' immigration records (1865-1919). The online immigration database was created by the Pier 21 Society from an existing series of name indexes, while the Home Children database is being produced by the British Isles Family History Society of Greater Ottawa, both societies working with the National Archives of Canada.

CANADIAN IMMIGRATION RECORDS DATABASE (1925-1935)

To search for an immigrant from the ArchiviaNet page, bring up the 'Immigration Records' screen and click on 'Search the database'. This will cause a search screen to display with several search boxes, into which you can enter the person's surname, given name (forename), year and port of arrival, and the name of the ship. You can enter data in all of the boxes, or choose only one, if you wish, and then click on 'Submit query'.

A list of database entries that match the search terms will then be displayed, with columns showing the immigrant's:

- surname;
- given name;
- age;
- nationality (which includes 'Scottish');
- year of arrival.

If you click on the 'entry' box to the left on the surname, a page will display, which gives even more information about the person, namely his or her:

- surname;
- given name;
- age;
- sex;

- nationality;
- date of arrival;
- port of arrival;
- ship.

In addition, the National Archives of Canada class reference, volume, page and microfilm reel of the original document are shown. The Immigration Records database also contains information on immigrants entering from the United States in the same ten-year period, where their surnames begin with the letter 'C'.

CANADIAN HOME CHILDREN DATABASE

In the 19th century thousands of British children began to be sent from children's homes to work on farms in Canada and Australia, which at that time were parts of the British Empire. Whether it was felt that the children would have a better life in the dominions than they'd have had in Britain, or whether it was simply a way of getting rid of unwanted pauper children who were a drain on the tax- and rate-payers, is open to debate. The emigration from Britain was done in many cases, however, without the children's consent. Most of them were orphans, but not all. Over 100,000 such children were sent to Canada, many of them Scottish.

To search for a home child in the database, click on 'Home Children' on the ArchiviaNet page and, when the page displays, click on 'Search the database'. Like the Immigration Records search screen, the screen that appears contains search boxes for surname, given name, year of arrival and ship. In addition, there's a search box for 'keywords', into which you can enter (for example) the name of a sending or destination organisation. These names don't always appear in the database records, however.

After you click on 'Submit query', a list of matching entries is displayed, showing for each child his or her:

- surname;
- given name;
- age;
- sex;
- ship;
- year of arrival.

As with the list of immigrants, if you click on the 'entry' box to the left of the surname, a page displays with more detailed information for that particular child, namely:

- surname;
- given name;
- age;
- sex;
- year of arrival;
- microfilm reel;
- ship;
- port of departure;
- departure date;
- port of arrival;
- arrival date;
- party;
- destination.

AUSTRALIAN IMMIGRATION INDEXES

Access to some of the family history records that are held by the Australian state governments of New South Wales, Tasmania and Victoria is now provided through their websites.

Cyndi's List of Genealogy Sites on the Internet (started by American family historian Cyndi Howells in 1996, and now containing over 200,000 links to family history websites) lists over 60 immigration indexes at www.cyndislist.com/austnz. htm#Ships, apart from those mentioned below.

NEW SOUTH WALES

The website of the State Records Authority of New South Wales www.records.nsw. gov.au hosts the following online indexes:

- 1841 Census (contains 9,354 entries);
- Assisted immigrants:
  - arriving at Port Phillip (1839-1851);
  - arriving in Sydney and Newcastle (1844-1859);
  - arriving at Moreton Bay, Brisbane (1848-1859);
  - arriving in Sydney (1860-1879);
  - arriving in Sydney (1880-1896).
- Bench of Magistrates cases, 1788-1820 (over 3,000 entries, including criminal and civil cases, publicans' licenses issued/cancelled, constables appointed, controlling markets etc.);
- Colonial Secretary Papers, 1788-1825 (listing a large number of names);
- Convicts:
  - Index to certificates of freedom (1823-1869);
  - Index to convict bank accounts (1837-1870);
  - Index to convict exiles (1849-50);
  - Index to pardons (1791-1825 and 1837-1841);
  - Index to tickets of exemption from government labor (1827-1832);
  - Index to tickets of leave, certificates of emancipation and pardons (1810-1819);
  - Index to ticket of leave passports (1835-1869).
- Gaol Photographs (over 20,000 covered by the index);
- Land records (includes maps and plans, 1792-1886, surveyors' letters, 1822-55, and surveyors' field books, 1794-1831);
- Naturalisation records (1834-1903);
- Quarter Sessions cases (1824-1837) – criminal and civil cases;
- Randwick Asylum for Destitute Children, 1852-1875 and 1885-1914 (over 4,000 entries);
- School records, admission registers, etc. (1876-1979);
- Shipping records (mainly for the 1870s).

Results of a search of the New South Wales Immigrant Index (1860-1879).

The actual records covered by the above indexes can, in most cases, be ordered from the website. The Assisted Immigrants indexes list:

- Family name;
- First name;
- Age;
- Ship;
- Year;
- Remarks (such as 'and family', 'and wife', etc.).

TASMANIA

Although the Archives Office of Tasmania doesn't host any online immigration records, it *does* provide Web access to a number of other genealogical indexes at www.archives.tas.gov.au/genealres/default.htm. These include indexes to:

- Tasmanian wills (1824-1948);
- Census records (1837, 1838, 1842, 1843, 1848, 1851 and 1857);

- Naturalisation applications (1835-1905);

- Applications by convicts for permission to marry (1829-1857).

In addition, the Archives Office has provided online access to a Colonial Tasmanian Family Links database, linking individuals with other members of their families living in Tasmania in the 19th century. The Archives Office stresses that the database, which contains around 500,000 entries, is designed to provide an *initial* online genealogical research resource.

The information in the database is based on records of births, marriages and deaths, as well as other events, held in the Archives Office of Tasmania, and the linkages have been developed by family historians associated with the National Heritage Foundation, an Australia-based charitable organisation that's developing an 'Applied Ancestry' project, on the basis that intimate knowledge of our ancestors allows all of us, and especially at-risk youth, to evaluate and manage our lives better.

All of the records covered by the Tasmanian indexes, together with those used in the Family Links database, can be ordered from the Archives Office by email.

VICTORIA

The Public Record Office Victoria provides access at www.prov.vic.gov.au/access. htm to indexes of:

- Assisted British Immigrants (1839-1871);

- Unassisted Immigration to Victoria from British and other ports (1852-1911).

These indexes list almost the same information as the New South Wales Assisted Immigrants indexes, but with the month of embarkation, and without the remarks.

6 UK National Archives
Soldiers' Discharge Papers Index

INTRODUCTION

The National Archives of the UK (TNA), formed in 2003 by the merger of the Public Record Office (PRO) and the Historical Manuscripts Commission, holds papers for soldiers in the British Army who were discharged to pension, many of whom were Scots. The records cover the years 1760 to 1913 and are held in the record class TNA: PRO WO 97 (where 'WO' stands for 'War Office'). An index of these WO 97 records can be searched over the Internet via PROCAT (Public Record Office Online Catalogue).

The records covered by the index are for the so-called 'other ranks': privates (in the infantry), troopers (in the cavalry), and the non-commissioned officers (NCOs) promoted from their ranks (i.e. sergeants and corporals). Commissioned officers are not included in the index. Although the actual records themselves are not available via PROCAT, they can be ordered online through the TNA website.

ACCESSING THE WO 97 INDEX VIA PROCAT

The PROCAT index is accessible at catalogue.pro.gov.uk (there is no 'www' in the website address). First click on the 'Search the catalogue' button, which will cause a search page to display on your screen. In box 1, key in the name of the soldier you're searching for, with 'AND' between his forename and surname (e.g. 'Alexander AND Stewart'), in box 3, enter 'WO 97', and click on the 'search' button. If your search is successful, this will cause one or more pages of results to be displayed, which you can then sort by 'covering dates' (i.e. start and end years of service). If you want to restrict the search, you can enter a range of dates in box 2.

According to the Edinburgh parish register, my 3x great-grandfather Alexander Stewart was a soldier in the '9th R.V.B.' stationed at Edinburgh Castle when he married in 1813 (see Chapter 3). A search for 'Alexander AND Stewart' with service between 1810 and 1820 produces a list of 16 different soldiers named 'Alexander Stewart' whose covering dates are wholly or partially within that period. The list shows for each man his:

- WO 97 reference number;
- name;
- place of birth;

- regiments served in;
- age at discharge;
- dates of service.

For my 3x great-grandfather, the index entry reads:

WO 97/1135/256
ALEXANDER STEWART Born DURINESS, Inverness-shire
Served in 3rd Garrison Battalion; 71st Foot Regiment; Lochaber Fencibles; 9th Royal
 Veteran Battalion
Discharged aged 36
Covering dates: 1798-1814

This is useful information in itself. The 9th Royal Veteran Battalion is the '9th R.V.B.' of the marriage record. Until I saw this listing, I had not been aware that any of my ancestors came from Duriness (usually called Duirinish), a parish in the north-western corner of the Isle of Skye. There was more information, however, in the actual records themselves.

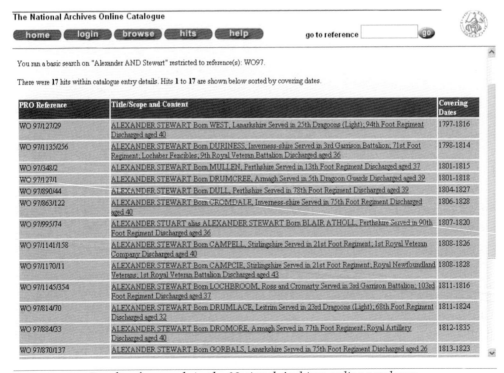

Results of a search in the National Archives online catalogue.

ORDERING DOCUMENTS FROM THE NATIONAL ARCHIVES

To order records online from The National Archives, you need to go to the web-site www.pro.gov.uk, and click on 'quick order'. When the Quick Order page displays, click on the highlighted text labelled 'Record Copying'. On the Record Copying page that then appears, you need to click on 'order form', and a page headed 'Request an Estimate' will be displayed.

It's the policy of The National Archives to issue a formal estimate before they'll carry out any record copying, so you have to apply for this first. There is a charge for the estimate (see Appendix 1), which covers up to five 'pieces' (items with a separate reference number), and is non-refundable. This is, in effect, the minimum charge for copying, and you pay more for your copies only if their cost exceeds the charge for the estimate.

On the 'Request an Estimate' page, you enter the full piece numbers for the items to be copied in as many of the five 'Piece Reference' boxes as you need to, and click the 'continue' button at the foot of the page. (In my case, the reference was 'WO 97/1135/256' from the list of soldiers.) Then complete the 'Customer Details' information on the second 'Request an Estimate' page, and click the 'continue' button.

A 'Summary' page will display, showing details of your order and address for confirmation, and tell you the cost of the estimate. Clicking on the 'Enter payment details' button at the bottom of the page will then take you to a secure payment site, where you can pay for the estimate by credit or debit card.

After about ten days The National Archives will send you an email message, letting you know the estimate is ready, with a link to an area of the TNA website with details of the cost of your potential copying order. If you want to go ahead with it you can pay for that online too. The records you want to see will then be copied and sent to you by post.

The copies can be either black and white on paper, 35mm microfilm, and 105mm microfiche, or colour on paper. In addition, you can receive digital copies of documents by post on CD-ROM, or over the Internet through TNA's *DocumentsOnline* (formerly PRO-Online) website (www.documentsonline.pro.gov.uk).

SOLDIERS' DISCHARGE DETAILS

The main item I received among the discharge papers for Alexander Stewart was his discharge certificate: an A3 printed form on which details of his service had been written by hand (shown below in a different typeface). It read as follows:

> His Majesty's 9th Royal Regiment of veterans, whereof General Colin Mackenzie is Colonel,
>
> These are to certify, that Alexander Stewart Private in Captn. Chisholm's Company in the Regiment aforesaid, born in the Parish of Duriness in or near the Town of Duriness

in the County of *Inverness*, was enlisted at the age of *20* Years; and hath served in the said Regiment for the space of *One* Year and *261* Days, as well as in other Corps, after the age of Eighteen, according to the following statement, but in consequence of *HRH the Prince Regent's Warrant for disbandment, Asthma, injd. Right leg, Cape of Good Hope,* is rendered unfit for further Service, and is hereby Discharged; having first received all just Demands of Pay, Clothing, &c. from his entry into the said Regiment to the Date of this Discharge, as appears by Receipt on the back hereof.

And to prevent any improper use being made of this Discharge, by its falling into other Hands, the following is a Description of the said *Private Alexr. Stewart*. He is about *36* Years of Age, is *5* Feet *7* Inches in height, *Brown* Hair, *Hazle* Eyes, *Fresh* Complexion, by Trade a *Weaver*.

Then came the 'Statement of Service', showing that Alexander Stewart had spent a total of 16 years and 28 days in the Army, as well as stating the exact dates on which he'd joined and left the four different regiments he'd served in. The form contains columns for the years and days spent in the ranks of private, corporal, sergeant, quarter-master sergeant and sergeant major, as well as time spent in the East or West Indies.

At the bottom of the page the certificate reads:

Given under my Hand and Seal of the Regiment at *Edinburgh Castle* the *12*th Day of *August 1814*.

Alexr. Rose Major
Commg. 9th R.V. Battn.

FIRST WORLD WAR CAMPAIGN MEDAL INDEX

At the beginning of 2004 the National Archives began putting information online about the campaign medals awarded during the First World War. The medal index is accessible via TNA's *Documents Online* website (see Chapter 16).

7 East India Company Indexes

INTRODUCTION

From 1600 until 1858 the East India Company was a major trading company, which not only employed many 'civil servants' – the origin of the term – but also maintained its own army to protect its trading posts in India. The East India Company's army, which was not part of the British Army, helped the company to expand from running a few trading posts to ruling most of India, which was divided into three large 'presidencies': Bengal (with Calcutta as its capital), Madras and Bombay.

Then, in 1857, came the Indian Mutiny, a major uprising of native soldiers in the north of the country. Most of the Company's troops were regiments of native infantry and cavalry, commanded by British officers and non-commissioned officers. The Mutiny of 1857 was not the first time troops had mutinied in India, but the earlier events had been localised and concerned with matters like pay and conditions. Indian historians tend to consider the Mutiny part of the struggle for independence from British rule.

Some of the native troops in Bengal mutinied because they were worried that the grease they were being issued to clean their rifles with was made from what their religions considered unclean animals. Hindus were concerned that the grease contained fat from cows, and Muslims that it was pig fat.

The British officers paid little attention to the soldiers' concerns until it was too late and British men, women and children had been massacred by the mutineers. The Mutiny was put down with equal brutality, the East India Company troops put under the command of the British Army, and the Company wound down.

The large part of India that had been controlled by the East India Company was placed under the British Crown from 1858 (until it gained independence in 1947 as the two countries of India and Pakistan), and Queen Victoria was crowned 'Empress of India'. By the time India regained its independence, the British had spent roughly the same length of time in India (350 years) as Britain had been part of the Roman Empire.

EAST INDIA COMPANY RECORDS

The records of the East India Company are held in the British Library in London, and include copies of the baptisms, marriages and burials of Europeans in India from the parish registers of the churches in the East India Company's three presidencies. Not all of these Europeans were British: the French, Dutch and Portuguese had also established trading posts on the Indian coast (indeed, Goa remained Portuguese and Pondicherry French until 1962).

These 'Ecclesiastical Returns' were sent to Company headquarters at East India House in the City of London. There are also various military records, such as muster rolls, embarkation lists and discharge papers, as well monumental inscriptions, wills (although some wills were proved in the Prerogative Court of Canterbury (PCC) in London – see Chapter 16), letters, ships' logs, etc.

Many Scots were in the service of the East India Company, which I first became aware of when I received the marriage certificate of my great-grandparents, William Brockman Stewart and Agnes Craig. The occupation of William's father, Alexander Stewart, was given as 'East India Company's Pensioner'. Much searching in the East India Company records led me to Alexander's wife, Alicia Elizabeth Wiltshire, and three more generations before her. It turned out that at least four of my ancestors of European origin (a Wiltshire, two Godfreys and an Adamson) had spent their entire lives in Madras. I also found that one of the four, Samuel Godfrey, was baptised in 1786 as the 'natural son' of a British officer. His mother was not mentioned in the entry in the parish records of St Mary's Church in Fort St George, Madras. I discovered that it was normal practice at the time to baptise illegitimate children of unions of European men and Indian women (without naming the women, who were not Christian), so my 5x great-grandmother was almost certainly Indian (probably Tamil).

There are several websites where you can find indexes to some of the East India Company's records.

THE INDIAMAN MAGAZINE INDEXES

On the website of *The Indiaman Magazine* (www.indiaman.com), you'll find various free search facilities. These include the first phase of a project indexing Bengal marriages (and some that took place in Madras) from a database of 20,000 entries based on the records held in the British Library's Oriental & India Office Collection (OIOC). You can search by entering either the bridegroom's surname, the bride's maiden surname, or the year in which the marriage took place. You can also order a photocopy of the actual record via the *Indiaman* website.

In addition, there is a database of 2,000 students who attended Haileybury College, which is near Hertford in England, and was founded by the East India Company in 1806. The information in the database includes the person's school career, time spent in India, and date and place of death. A third searchable database lists over 15,000 names being researched by readers of *The Indiaman Magazine*.

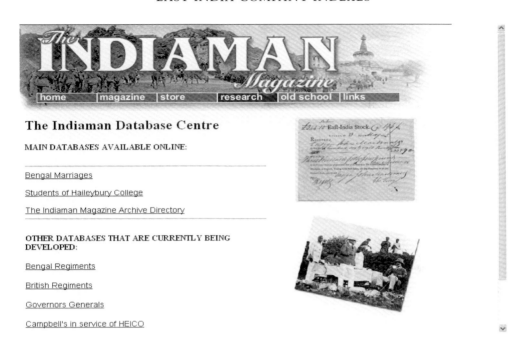

Page on The Indiaman Magazine *website, listing several databases.*

Other databases that are currently being developed include those for Bengal regiments, British regiments, Governors-General, Campbells in the service of the East India Company, and monumental inscriptions. Paul Rowland, editor of *The Indiaman Magazine*, hoped to have some, if not all, of these additional databases available for searching via the *Indiaman* website during 2004.

FAMILY HISTORY IN INDIA INDEXES

On the *Family History in India* website (members.ozemail.com.au/~clday/index. html) of Cathy Day of Canberra, Australia, there is also a database of Bengal marriages from 1855-1864 and 1874-1896, which have also been transcribed from the original records in the OIOC. Note that there's no 'www' in the address of Cathy's website, which is an absolute mine of information for anyone with East India Company or British India connections.

INDEX TO CADET PAPERS

An index of men who were officer cadets of the East India Company between 1789 and 1859 is available on the *Genealogy in India* pages of the website of Bob Holland (www.ans.com.au/~rampais/genelogy/india/index.htm), also in Australia. Yes, the address really does contain the word 'genelogy' without the 'a' in the middle!

Bob's officer cadet index provides the relevant OIOC reference number and LDS Family History Centre microfilm number. These numbers enable you to order the films containing the relevant records from the nearest LDS Family History Centre (see Chapter 9), where they can then be viewed.

Among other Indian-related lists and indexes on Bob's website is a list of Scots who went out to India. This was transcribed by Pauline McGregor Currien, who extracted names with a possible Indian connection from a series of booklets entitled *Emigrants from Glasgow and the West of Scotland*, published by the Scottish Genealogy Society (see Appendix 5).

INTERNATIONAL GENEALOGICAL INDEX

You can also find births, marriages and deaths of Europeans in India through the International Genealogical Index (IGI) on the LDS *FamilySearch* website (www. familysearch.org) (see Chapter 9).

8 Miscellaneous Indexes

SCOTTISH STRAYS MARRIAGE INDEX

This is an online index of marriages that took place (mainly) outside Scotland, where at least one of the spouses was born in Scotland. The index was compiled by the Anglo-Scottish Family History Society (ASFHS), a specialist branch of the Manchester & Lancashire Family History Society (M&LFHS).

The ASFHS was founded in 1982 to help M&LFHS members trace their Scottish ancestors, and has membership in the USA, Canada, Australia and New Zealand. In addition to creating the Marriage Index, the ASFHS has also published five volumes of information on Scots who migrated to England and Wales, as well as a digest of sources for Scottish family history at Manchester Central Library.

The Marriage Index, which can be used free of charge at the M&LFHS Web site (www.m&lfhs.org.uk), lists for each spouse his or her:

- surname;
- forename(s);
- date of birth;
- place of birth;
- parents' names;
- spouse's name;
- location of the marriage;
- country (or county) where it took place;
- date of the marriage.

In addition, a 'source number' is given in most cases, so you can make contact (through the ASFHS) with the person who supplied the information. The society encourages users of the index to supply information on additional marriages, provided one of the partners was born in Scotland.

To view the index, you need to have on your computer the Acrobat Reader program, which can be downloaded free of charge from Adobe Systems (www.adobe.com). To search for a name, first click on one of the index groups (for example, 'A to B') on the web page.

Once Acrobat Reader has opened and the first page of that particular file is displayed on screen, you can click on the 'bookmarks' tab on the left, which will let you see further index groups within the larger group. You can then click on one of those (for example, 'Bell to Bock') to navigate closer to the name you're looking for. Note that 'Mac' and 'Mc' names are not listed together, but in strict alphabetical order. Some of the entries in the Marriage Index are more helpful than others. In a number of cases, the place of birth is given as simply 'Scotland', while in others, there is no information at all about the person's birthdate, birthplace or parents.

Unfortunately, lack of space seems to have led to truncation of some of the information. Where the county code is given, you can probably identify the place of marriage. Where the code is simply 'SCT' (for Scotland), however, you may need to check with the information provider to see whether the 'E' in 'St Cuthberts, E' (for example) stands for 'Edinburgh' (which it probably does, as St Cuthberts was a large parish there) or some other place name beginning with the letter 'E' (such as 'Elgin').

COMMONWEALTH WAR GRAVES COMMISSION INDEX

The Commonwealth War Graves Commission (CWGC) was set up in 1917 (as the Imperial War Graves Commission), thanks to the efforts of Fabian Ware, an educationalist and newspaper editor. At 45, Ware was considered too old for military service, and went to France in September 1914 in command of a mobile Red Cross unit.

Seeing that no-one was responsible for marking and recording soldiers' graves, Ware took on this responsibility for his unit. In 1915 the British Government recognised the value of his work by setting up a Graves Registration Commission within the Army, with Ware in command in the rank of Major. By the end of the war he had been promoted to Major-General, and in 1920 became Sir Fabian Ware.

The CWGC marks and maintains the graves of the 1.7 million members of the armed forces of Commonwealth countries who were killed in the two World Wars, and builds memorials for those who have no known grave. The Commission also keeps records and registers listing those killed, including the Civilian War Dead of the Second World War.

These records have now been made available for searching over the Internet. To find information on an ancestor or relative who died in either of the world wars, you enter his or her surname in the search box on the Commission's home page (www.cwgc.org).

Beware that searching for a 'Mac' surname will not find those beginning with 'Mc', although using an asterisk as a wildcard character (i.e. 'M*c') will find both. To cut down the number of names listed, it's best to enter the person's initial as well. There's no facility to key in a forename, but you can enter a second initial, provided you separate the two initials with a space. The CWGC warns against using full stops or following the second initial with a space.

You'll probably know in which war the person was killed, so you can select either 'World War 1' or 'World War 2' from the pull-down menu. You can select a range of years from the next two pull-down menus, or if you know the year of death, select the same year in both cases. To restrict the search still further, you can select the force (from 'Army', 'Air Force', 'Navy', 'Merchant Navy', and 'Civilian') and/or nationality (from 'Australian', 'Canadian', 'Indian', 'New Zealand', 'South African' and 'United Kingdom'. This is the nationality of the fighting force, rather than the individual.

Then click on the 'search' button, and a list of individuals who meet the criteria will be displayed. Click on one of those names and a 'Casualty Details' screen will appear, showing the following information about the deceased person:

- full name;
- initials;
- nationality;
- rank;
- regiment;
- unit of the regiment;
- age (if known);

- date of death;
- service number;
- additional information (such as parents' names);
- casualty type (military or civilian);
- grave/memorial reference;
- name of cemetery.

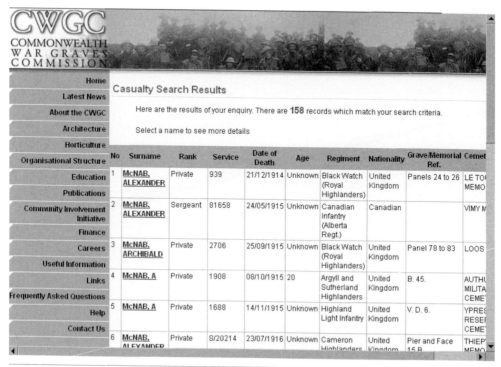

Results of a casualty search.

On the casualty details screen, you can click on the 'view details' button next to the name of the cemetery to find out where it's located, when it was erected, and how many people are buried there. Alternatively, if you click on the 'certificate' button, the details are printed out in the form:

In Memory of
Private JAMES ALFRED SMITH
201508, 4th Bn., Royal Scots
who died
on 19 April 1917
Private SMITH
Remembered with honour
JERUSALEM MEMORIAL
[then follows a colour photograph of the cemetery]
Commemorated in perpetuity by
the Commonwealth War Graves Commission

GRETNA GREEN INDEX

Over the years many English people have gone to Scotland to marry, mainly because it was (and still is) possible to marry there without parental consent at an earlier age than in England. Even today, when you have to be 18 to marry without your parents' permission in England, there is no need for such consent to marry in Scotland, once you've turned 16.

This difference made Scotland an attractive place of marriage for English couples, where one or both were under age. Under Lord Hardwicke's Marriage Act of 1754, parental consent was required if either of the parties to the marriage was under 21. The Act did not apply to Scotland, however, where it was then possible to marry merely by making a declaration before two witnesses. Couples tended to marry at Gretna Green, Lamberton Toll, and a few other places, because they were close to the English border.

After 1856 you had to be resident in Scotland for three weeks to be able to marry there. This residence qualification meant that eloping couples could be followed by irate parents and stopped before it was too late, and so elopements to Gretna Green and other places just over the border died out.

An index of around 4,500 irregular marriages that took place at Gretna Green between 1795 and 1895 (and also those for a few years earlier) can be searched free of charge on the website of Achievements Ltd. of Canterbury, England (www. achievements.co.uk/services/gretna/index.php). Achievements, a not-for-profit genealogical research company, is the commercial arm of the Institute for Heraldic & Genealogical Studies, the first UK school for the study of the history and structure of the family and allied subjects. Having found a marriage that you're interested in, you can then order and pay via the Achievements website to receive full details of the marriage as given in the register. (See Appendix 1.)

But, you may be thinking, surely the names contained in the Gretna Green database will all be those of English people, rather than Scots? You would think so, wouldn't you? A search for names beginning with the prefix 'Mac' or 'Mc' brings up 30 matches, however. In addition, there are 142 Scotts, 57 Murrays, 29 Fergusons or Fergussons, 18 Campbells, 17 Stewarts or Stuarts, 8 Rosses, and 5 Robertsons in the index.

A list of custodians and owners of all the known existing records of Scottish Irregular and Runaway Marriages (at Gretna and various other places) can be seen on the General Register Office for Scotland (GROS) website at www.gro-scotland.gov. uk/grosweb/grosweb.nsf/pages/runmar. This list is based on one originally compiled in 1927 by G.W. Shirley of the Ewart Library in Dumfries, extended by George Crighton, and later further extended by Ronald Nicholson.

Interestingly, the number of marriages in Gretna has risen again over the last 20 years, with 5,278 marriages (17.4 per cent of the 30,367 marriages in Scotland) taking place there in 2000. Very few of these modern Gretna marriages involve young people, however. According to a paper on 'Marriages at Gretna, 1975-2000' by G.W.L. Jackson, published on the Web in August 2001 by the GROS at www.gro-scotland. gov.uk/grosweb/grosweb.nsf/pages/occpgg, only 4.4 per cent of marriages in Gretna in 2000 involved someone under 21, and only 1.2 per cent someone under 18. In fact, the average ages of brides and grooms were 33 and 36 respectively.

Over 72 per cent of the people marrying at Gretna in 2000 were resident in England, with 14 per cent in Scotland, 4.5 per cent in Wales, and 3 per cent in Northern Ireland. About 6 per cent of brides and 5 per cent of grooms came from outside the UK, with the main countries of origin being the Irish Republic, the United States, the Netherlands, Australia, Germany, France, Canada, Belgium, Switzerland, and Sweden.

POLICE INDEX

Not all indexes of genealogical information have been set up by government departments, official bodies, or family history societies: some have been put in place by enthusiastic amateurs (in the best sense of the word). One of these people is Derek Wilcox, who has created a number of indexes, including those covering police and 'black sheep', that you can access free of charge on his website (www. lightage.demon.co.uk).

The Police Index contains the names of over 70,000 police officers mentioned in British newspaper reports spanning the period 1860-1920 – and many of these officers are Scottish. The reports may include biographies and photographs, as well as information on cases, careers, presentations, obituaries and service in the Boer War and First World War.

The index lists the:

- police officer's name;
- forename;
- rank;
- police force;
- reason he or she is mentioned in the newspaper;
- the year of the report.

BLACK SHEEP INDEX

The other main index on Derek's site is the Black Sheep Index (BSI) of 90,000 other people mentioned in newspaper reports of court cases and inquests between 1860 and 1900. Derek points out himself, however, that not all of those included in the database are 'black sheep' (i.e. criminals, etc.). The court cases and inquests reported on relate to murder, suicide, assault, accident, divorce, disaster, fraud, probate, cruelty and theft. Many of the people listed in the BSI are Scottish.

The BSI lists a person's:

- name;
- forename;
- age;
- occupation or relationship;
- address/town;
- the year of the report.

If all of the above information wasn't in the newspaper, then it won't be in the index either. Age and occupation, in particular, are often missing.

OTHER INDEXES

Derek's website also provides access to other smaller indexes, such as the World War II Index, which covers over 4,000 members of the Allied Forces mentioned in articles in British magazines about the Second World War. The articles include stories of Royal Navy and Merchant Navy ships, and histories of RAF Squadrons and Army Regiments. A Roll of Honour lists photographs of those who were killed, usually with brief details.

Another index lists police officers who were awarded medals by the Liverpool Shipwreck & Humane Society (LSHS), which was founded in 1839 with the aim of rewarding people who saved lives. The index includes winners of the society's marine, fire and general medals, the latter being awarded for acts of bravery other than marine and fire rescues.

The site also contains an index of Manchester police officers in 1877, whose records may be available from the Manchester Police Museum. Although Liverpool and Manchester are in England, you'll find a number of Scottish names in both indexes, as well as in the World War II Index.

Derek has also included on his website a Victorian Index, which is really three separate indexes: of people endorsing products (usually patent medicines) in advertisements, theatrical people, and sportsmen. The Victorian Theatre Index covers actors, actresses, Music Hall entertainers, and 'other people in the Victorian theatre'. There are entries for the French actress Sarah Bernhardt and the English Music Hall star Dan Leno ('the funniest man on Earth'), as well as for lesser lights such as the (Scottish?) lady wrestler Florence Stuart.

For the people whose names are held in the various indexes, Derek will send you a copy of the relevant newspaper report for a small fee. (See Appendix 1.)

9 More Family History Websites, Mailing Lists and Discussion Groups

A. LDS *FAMILYSEARCH*

Members of the Church of Jesus Christ of Latter-day Saints (the 'Mormons') believe their ancestors can be re-united with their living families through covenants in LDS temples. To be able to make the covenants, the LDS members have to identify their ancestors first. This is the reason their church is so active in genealogical research, which it kindly makes available to other people free of charge.

As long ago as 1894, the LDS church founded the Genealogical Society of Utah (GSU) to help church members with their family history research and to provide a library of genealogical material. The Family History Library (previously the Genealogical Library) has long made use of new technology in its handling of genealogical data: in 1938 it began to use microfilm, and 60 years later held over two million rolls of microfilmed records. The master copies of these rolls are kept in the Granite Mountain Records Vault, which was tunnelled into the mountainside in 1963 around 25 miles from Salt Lake City, Utah.

Fifty years after its founding, the GSU's articles of incorporation expired, and the society became a church corporation: the Genealogical Society of the Church of Jesus Christ of Latter-day Saints, which became the Genealogical Department in 1975. A change of name to the Family History Department followed in 1987, and the department was combined with the church's Historical Department in 2000 as the Family and Church History Department.

The church's Genealogical Library kept outgrowing its accommodation in Salt Lake City during the 20th century, eventually moving into its own specially designed library building in 1985. Two years later it became the Family History Library, which was felt to be a more 'user-friendly' name. The library is now used by around 2,500 people per day.

The International Genealogical Index

One of the most useful of the LDS indexes is the International Genealogical Index (IGI), which used to be available on microfiche, then CD-ROM, and is now on the Web at www.familysearch.org. The IGI is an index of births/baptisms, marriages/banns, and deaths/burials of people in many countries of the world. (Scotland,

Search page for the International Genealogical Index (IGI) on the LDS FamilySearch website. (Reprinted by permission. Copyright © 1999-2002, by Intellectual Reserve, Inc.)

International Genealogical Index / British Isles - 11

Select records to download - (50 maximum)

1. JOHN LITTLE - International Genealogical Index
   Gender: Male Birth: 24 SEP 1833 Saint Cuthberts, Edinburgh, Midlothian, Scotland
2. JANET LITTLE - International Genealogical Index
   Gender: Female Birth: 07 FEB 1825 Saint Cuthberts, Edinburgh, Midlothian, Scotland
3. MARGARET DRUMMOND LITTLE - International Genealogical Index
   Gender: Female Birth: 16 MAY 1830 Saint Cuthberts, Edinburgh, Midlothian, Scotland
4. MARGARET CARNEGIE LITTLE - International Genealogical Index
   Gender: Female Birth: 02 DEC 1831 Saint Cuthberts, Edinburgh, Midlothian, Scotland
5. ALEXANDER LITTLE - International Genealogical Index
   Gender: Male Christening: 05 AUG 1819 Saint Cuthberts, Edinburgh, Midlothian, Scotland
6. ANDREW LITTLE - International Genealogical Index
   Gender: Male Birth: 14 SEP 1828 Saint Cuthberts, Edinburgh, Midlothian, Scotland
7. CHARLES LITTLE - International Genealogical Index
   Gender: Male Birth: 13 OCT 1826 Saint Cuthberts, Edinburgh, Midlothian, Scotland
8. DAVID THOMSON LITTLE - International Genealogical Index
   Gender: Male Christening: 19 APR 1816 Saint Cuthberts, Edinburgh, Midlothian, Scotland
9. WILLIAM LITTLE - International Genealogical Index
   Gender: Male Christening: 26 MAY 1818 Saint Cuthberts, Edinburgh, Midlothian, Scotland
10. MARY LITTLE - International Genealogical Index
    Gender: Female Birth: 30 MAY 1823 Saint Cuthberts, Edinburgh, Midlothian, Scotland
11. NICOLAS LITTLE - International Genealogical Index
    Gender: Female Birth: 24 JAN 1821 Saint Cuthberts, Edinburgh, Midlothian, Scotland

prev | next   Prepare selected records for download

Results of a search in the IGI, specifying only the parents' names. (Reprinted by permission. Copyright © 1999-2002, by Intellectual Reserve, Inc.)

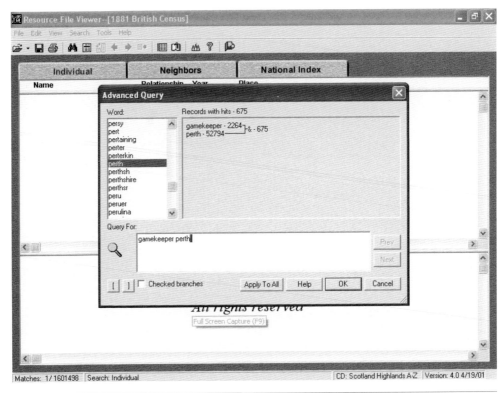

Advanced search in the 1881 census on the LDS CD-ROM, looking for gamekeepers in Perth. (Reprinted by permission. Copyright © 1999, by Intellectual Reserve, Inc.)

England, Wales, Ireland, the Isle of Man and the Channel Islands are all considered to be different countries on the IGI.)

The IGI consists of names which have either been extracted from official documents or input by members of the LDS church. In Scotland's case, the extracted names come from the Old Parish Registers and the statutory records from 1855-1875.

To carry out a search on the IGI, click on the 'Search' tab or the 'Search for your ancestors in our vast record collections' link. On the page that then displays, click on 'International Genealogical Index' on the left-hand side of the page. The IGI search page will then appear. Select 'British Isles' for 'region', 'Scotland' for 'country', and if you wish, you can also select the name of the county.

Compared to spending credits looking for your ancestors in the *ScotlandsPeople* indexes (www.scotlandspeople.gov.uk), searching in the IGI is free of charge. In addition, you can search for all the children of a couple by selecting the region and country (and county, if you wish) and entering only the parents' names. This facility is not available via *ScotlandsPeople*.

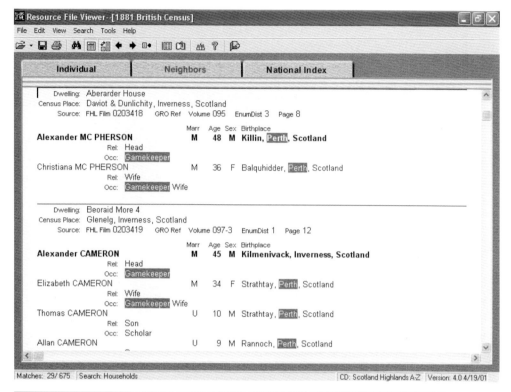

Some of the results of a search for gamekeepers in Perth in the LDS 1881 census CD-ROM. (Reprinted by permission. Copyright © 1999, by Intellectual Reserve, Inc.)

1880/1881 Censuses

Also available to search free of charge on the *FamilySearch* website is the British census of 1881 (as well as the US census of 1880 and Canadian census of 1881), but only for England, Wales, the Isle of Man and the Channel Islands. For the 1881 census for Scotland, you have to go to the *ScotlandsPeople* website and pay for access. Alternatively, you can buy the CD-ROM version of the 1881 British census from the LDS church, and then use it as often as you like – without paying any more money! With the CD-ROM set, you can also search for specific terms on each of the CDs, so you can look for all the gamekeepers or all the people born in India, which you can't do online.

LDS Family History Centres

Over 3,700 Family History Centres, which are branches of the LDS Family History Library, have been opened in around 90 countries. At any of the centres you can order microfilm copies of records, which are sent to the centre, where you can then make use of them. You don't have to be a member of the Church of Jesus Christ of Latter-day Saints to use the Family History Centres.

B. *GENUKI*

The *GENUKI* website (www.genuki.org.uk) was set up in 1995, in the fairly early days of the World Wide Web. Its stated aim is to act as a 'virtual reference library' of genealogical information about the United Kingdom and the Irish Republic, as well as the Isle of Man and the Channel Islands. The site is organised in different levels: as well as information relating to all of the British Isles at the top level, *GENUKI* consists of six sections at the next level: Scotland, England, Wales, Ireland, Isle of Man and Channel Islands.

At the level for the whole of Scotland, you'll find information on the following subjects:

- Archives and Libraries
- Bibliography
- Biography
- Cemeteries
- Census
- Chronology
- Church History
- Church Records
- Civil Registration
- Correctional Institutions
- Court Records
- Description and Travel
- Directories
- Emigration and Immigration
- Encyclopaedias and Dictionaries
- Gazetteers
- Genealogy
- Handwriting
- Historical Geography
- History
- Land and Property
- Language and Languages
- Law and Legislation
- Maps
- Merchant Marine
- Migration, Internal
- Military History
- Names, Geographical
- Names, Personal
- Newspapers
- Nobility
- Occupations
- Periodicals
- Poorhouses, Poor Law, etc.
- Population
- Probate Records
- Schools
- Social Life and Customs
- Societies
- Statistics
- Taxation

In addition, at the country level of *GENUKI* are links leading to pages with information on each of the 33 historic counties of Scotland (from Aberdeenshire to

GENUKI Home Page GENUKI Contents  Information related to all of the UK and Ireland Regions

THE UNITED KINGDOM AND IRELAND

The **UK and Ireland** are regarded, for the purposes of this Genealogical Information Service, as being made up of **England**, **Ireland** (i.e. *Northern Ireland* and the *Republic of Ireland*), **Wales**, and **Scotland**, together with the **Channel Islands** and the **Isle of Man**. Together, these constitute the *British Isles* - which is a geographical term for a group of islands lying off the north-west coast of mainland Europe. (Legally, the Channel Islands and the Isle of Man are largely self governing, and are not part of the United Kingdom.) The Administrative Regions into which the UK and Ireland are divided have changed frequently in recent years. However, in line with normal genealogical practice, this Information Service is structured according to the counties as shown in these maps of England, Scotland and Wales, and of Ireland, i.e., as they were prior to the re-organisation that took place in 1974 (1975 for Scotland).

REGIONS

- England
- Ireland
- Scotland

Ireland

Scotland

Isle of Man

- Wales
- Channel Islands
- Isle of Man

England

Wales

Channel Islands

France

GENUKI home page for the United Kingdom and Ireland.

Wigtownshire). These pages are also divided into similar categories to those for the entire country, minus those that don't apply to that particular county, but including folklore and obituaries. The county level has links leading to the parishes within the county with more information at that level.

How much detail there is at each level varies according to the particular area. Glasgow has far more information than the neighbouring Lanarkshire parish of Rutherglen; likewise Edinburgh. The parishes that are nowadays part of the large Edinburgh unitary authority are accessible via links on both the Midlothian and Edinburgh pages. (See Chapter 3.)

C. SCOTS ORIGINS

Between 1998 and 31 August 2002 online access to the indexes of General Register Office for Scotland (GROS) was provided by Origins.net through its *Scots Origins* website (www.scotsorigins.com). When continued provision of the service was put out to tender by GROS, the contract was won by Scotland On Line (SOL). In partnership with GROS, SOL has provided the *ScotlandsPeople* service since 1 September 2002. (See Chapters 1-3.)

The *Scots Origins* website continues to exist, however, and now provides a chargeable 'Sighting Service', free place-name search, and free enhanced searching in the LDS Church's International Genealogical Index (IGI).

Sighting Service

Using the *Scots Origins* Sighting Service, you can order transcripts of births, marriages and deaths from the GROS statutory records, baptisms/births and marriages/banns from the Old Parish Registers (OPRs), and entries from the 1861 and 1871 censuses. You can place your order via the *Scots Origins* website, and receive your transcriptions within 10 working days. If you have an email address, they'll be sent to you over the Internet. Otherwise, they'll be sent by post.

You may be wondering why anyone would want to order transcriptions of documents from *Scots Origins*, when they could view the actual images more cheaply on the *ScotlandsPeople* website. That's certainly the case with the OPRs and the censuses, although when the Sighting Service began in 2002 images of these records were not yet available to view online.

It's still the case, however, that the most recent statutory records are not available in image form on the Web. That means there's a cut-off point of 100 years for births, 75 years for marriages, and 50 years for deaths. To see records more recent that that you have to go to New Register House in Edinburgh – or get someone like *Scots Origins* to do it for you.

Scots Origins are not the only service that will do this for you. If you carry out a general online search (with a search-engine like Google) for 'Scottish family history research', you'll find a number of organisations that will do your Scottish research for you. With *Scots Origins*, however, you can make your payment online, and you don't have to make a large payment up-front.

To use the Sighting Service for statutory records, you'll need to supply *Scots Origins* with the following information:

- **for births:** full name of child, parents' names, year of child's birth (+/- 2 years), and Registration District;

- **for marriages:** full name of bride and bridegroom, year of marriage (+/- 5 years), and preferably Registration District;

- **for deaths:** full name, approximate age, year of death (+/- 5 years), and Registration District where the death occurred.

The information you'll be provided with through the sighting service is the same as you would get on an official certificate or on the online images available through *ScotlandsPeople* for older records. (See Chapter 1.)

Place-name Search

You can find the number of the Registration District by using the free search facility on *Scots Origins*. You can select the name of the county, or simply enter the name of the place you're looking for (which can be a town, village, street or farm). The counties and places are those in existence at the time of the 1881 census, so newer street names won't be found.

If you key in 'Dunrobin', for example, without specifying a county, you'll find in your results 'Dunrobin Castle' (home of the Dukes of Sutherland) in Golspie, Sutherland, as well as 'Dunrobin Glen' and 'Dunrobin Mains' in the same place. Also listed, however, are various Dunrobin streets, including 'Dunrobin Place' in Edinburgh.

Enhanced Searching in the IGI

The *Scots Origins* site lets you search the International Genealogical Index (IGI) on the LDS *FamilySearch* website on an individual parish basis (which you can't do on the *FamilySearch* site itself). You can also search by parish through a website provided by Hugh Wallis on his Web pages at RootsWeb (freepages.genealogy. rootsweb.com/~hughwallis/IGIBatchNumbers.htm). Note that there's no 'www' in the address. Hugh also provides an interesting middle-name index on his pages, where you can search for middle-names that are probably surnames, which may help you to identify additional members of your extended family.

D. MAILING LISTS, FORUMS AND DISCUSSION GROUPS

Mailing Lists

As well as the various websites mentioned so far, there are also many mailing lists devoted to Scottish family history. Being a member of a mailing list allows you to correspond with the other members of the group by e-mail. Once you've joined the list, any message you send to it will be sent to everyone else who's on the list. In turn, you'll receive all the messages that the other members send.

At RootsWeb (www.rootsweb.com), there are over 27,000 genealogy mailing lists. On the RootsWeb home page, if you click on 'Index' in the Mailing Lists section, that will take you to the main index page, which is divided into sections for Surnames, the USA, International, and Other (non-geographical) lists. In the International section, if you click on 'Scotland', you'll be taken to a page with an index of just over 250 mailing lists on Scottish subjects.

More than two-thirds of these lists are concerned with specific surnames. There are also mailing lists for all the historic Scottish counties, as well as Edinburgh, Glasgow and a few other areas. In addition, general Scottish subjects, such as the Jacobites, DNA, cemeteries, mining, medieval history and monumental inscriptions are represented in the index.

If you click on the name of the mailing list you're interested in, a page for that particular list will display, which enables you to subscribe (free of charge) to the list, and unsubscribe when you no longer want to receive messages. In addition, you can search or browse the archived messages for that list without having to join.

On busy lists, there can be very many messages arriving in your in-box, so you may prefer to subscribe to the digest version of the list, in which several messages are grouped together. The only problem with that is that you have to read the digest to see if it contains anything of interest to you, rather than checking by simply looking at the e-mail message headers.

Usenet Newsgroups

Usenet (an abbreviation of 'Users' Network') is the world's largest Internet bulletin board system, which was started in 1979 at Duke University in North Carolina in the United States. Users can post messages in forums known as 'newsgroups', which can be read using 'newsreader' programs such as Outlook Express and Agent. There are now many thousands of newsgroups, covering all sorts of different topics.

An archive of all the messages posted on Usenet since 1981 can be found at the website of the search-engine Google, in its Google Groups section (www.google.com/grphp). You can search the archive in the same way as you would web pages, and also make postings to newsgroups, without the need for newsreader software.

RootsWeb Message Boards

As well as mailing lists, RootsWeb also hosts over 132,000 message boards, on which you can post queries free of charge. These are grouped by surname or locality. For Scotland, there is a message board for each of the historic counties, as well as a general board for the whole of Scotland and one for the Western Isles. Messages posted to the boards are also sent to those subscribing to the equivalent RootsWeb mailing list.

ScotlandsPeople Discussion Group

On the *ScotlandsPeople* website there is a discussion group bulletin board at (www.scotlandspeople.gov.uk/phpBB/index.php) to which anyone can post messages free of charge. There are over 40 forums in five groups: News, Help, General Discussion, Records/Search, and Countries & Continents.

Yahoo! Groups

At the *Yahoo! UK & Ireland* website (uk.groups.yahoo.com) there are several family history discussion groups, including a number with Scottish-based themes. On the main *Yahoo!* Groups web page, click on 'Genealogy' in the 'Family & Home' section.

10 The Statistical Accounts of Scotland

INTRODUCTION

In the 1790s the Church of Scotland ministers of all the 938 church parishes in Scotland wrote accounts of what life was like for their parishioners. These are known as the Statistical Accounts of Scotland, and are not the dull-sounding documents you might expect from the title. The ministers wrote about the landscape, the crops that were grown, the fish to be found in the rivers and the sea, how much things cost, about the number of people living in the parish, and whether they spoke Gaelic or broad Scots.

Some of the ministers wrote fairly short accounts of their parishes, while others really went to town, writing very detailed descriptions of life at that time (and revealing their own views and prejudices in the process). Your ancestors are unlikely to be mentioned by name, but the statistical accounts provide a wonderful background to family history research.

The original Statistical Account of Scotland was the idea of Sir John Sinclair of Ulbster (1754-1835), Member of Parliament for Caithness and a lay member of the General Assembly of the Church of Scotland. Following a century and a half of failed attempts to produce a parish-by-parish 'Geographical Description of Scotland', the Statistical Account was published in 21 volumes between 1791 and 1799.

'My original intention was to have drawn up a General Statistical View of North Britain without any particular reference to parochial districts,' wrote Sir John in Volume 21, 'but I found such merit and ability, and so many important facts and useful observations, in the communications which were sent me, that I could not think of depriving the clergy of the credit they were entitled to derive from such laborious exertions.'

To assist the parish ministers in their task, Sir John gave them 160 questions to answer. The first 40 related to the geography and topography of the parish, including its climate, natural resources and natural history. Then followed 60 questions covering different aspects of the parish's population, and 16 on agricultural and industrial production, while the remainder dealt with miscellaneous topics.

A New Statistical Account of Scotland was published between 1834 and 1845, and a Third Statistical Account between 1951 and 1992. The New Statistical Account contained county maps, and the accounts of the parishes, although still written by the ministers, also included contributions from local doctors, teachers and landowners.

The first and second ('Old' and New) Statistical Accounts can be accessed online free of charge at (edina.ac.uk/statacc). Note that there's no 'www' in the address. You can also subscribe on an annual basis to an enhanced version of the service, which lets you search for information in either or both sets of accounts. The subscription service also allows you to see the accounts as text (rather than images of the original pages) that can be cut and pasted, and lets you download accounts of up to ten individual parishes per year as portable document format (pdf) files.

Here are some examples of the sort of information you can find in the Statistical Accounts.

COST OF LIVING

Details of the cost of living for a labourer's family were provided by the Reverend Alexander Stewart (not one of my Stewarts, as far as I know) in his account of the parish of Moulin, in Perthshire, in the 1790s:

> The following is an estimate of the expences and earnings of a labouring man, his wife, and four children, the eldest under eight years, the youngest an infant.
>
> Subsistence per week, 3 pecks of potatoes at 4 pence, 2 pecks of oatmeal at 11 pence, 2 pecks of bearmeal [barley] at 7½ pence, salt, milk, eggs, beer, etc. 6 pence; total 4 shillings 7 pence or £11:18:4 the year; from which, deducting 4 weeks subsistence of the man in harvest, at 1 shilling 10 pence the week, or 7 shillings 7 pence [in total], there remains £11:11:0.
>
> Rent of house and garden may be estimated at 15 shillings; fuel at 20 shillings; 12 carts of peat at 1 shilling; 8 carts of turf at 8 pence, heath or wood 2 shillings 8 pence; soap and blue for washing, at 4 shillings 6 pence; and oil for light at 2 shillings; total £2:1:6. The ashes will dung the garden, and pay the expence of digging and planting it with greens or potatoes.
>
> Man's clothing, coat at 5 shillings 9 pence, vest at 2 shillings 4 pence, the lining of the coat and vest, and back of the latter, made out of the wife's old clothes; breeches and hose 4 shillings, 2 pairs shoes 7 shillings, 2 shirts 6 shillings 9½ pence; also a great coat at 10 shillings, bonnet at 1 shilling, and handkerchief at 1 shilling 6 pence; these three last articles only once in two years, hence 6 shillings 3 pence; total £1:12:1½ the year.
>
> Wife's cloathing, gown and petticoats at 16 shillings 10½ pence, 2 shifts 5 shillings 7½ pence, hose 8 pence, 1 pair shoes 4 shillings, neck handkerchief 2 shillings, apron 1 shilling 6 pence, bodice 2 shillings 3 pence, this last article once in two years; hence 1 shilling 1½ pence; total £1:11:9½ the year.
>
> Children, 3 pairs shoes 5 shillings, jackets 13 shillings 2 pence, shirts 4 shillings 11 pence; total £1:3:1. Bed clothes and household furniture are supposed to be provided either before marriage, or soon after it. It is also supposed that the wife has provided

so much body clothes as will reduce the yearly expence of her own and the children's clothing one third. Hence the annual expence of clothing the family will be £3:8:9
Subsistence £11:11:0
House-rent, fuel, etc. £2:1:6
[Total] £17:1:3

The man earns in 26 weeks during spring and summer, at the rate of 6 shillings the week, £7:16:0
Four weeks in harvest (besides victuals), £1:6:0
Twenty-two weeks in autumn and winter, at 3 shillings 6 pence [the week], £3:17:0
[Total] £12:19:0

The wife earns by spinning or otherwise, 1 shilling the week, £2:12:0
(A woman who is a good spinner, and employed in nothing else, may earn 3 shillings the week; but 1 shilling is a high enough estimate of the earnings of a woman who has a family of 2 or 3 young children to take care of.)

[Grand Total] £15:11:0
Deficiency £1:10:3

Although there thus appears to be a deficiency of earnings, after the charges have been estimated in the most frugal, and even scanty manner, and no allowance made for casual expences; yet it is certain, that in this country, people who seem to have no livelihood but the fruits of their daily labour, do, by some means or other, bring up families and even give their children such education as the nearest school affords.

POPULATION

In the 'Old' account of the parish of Duirinish (on the Isle of Skye), Inverness-shire, the Revd William Bethune described how the population of the parish (and the whole island) had been increasing for at least the previous 80 years.

The old people affirm that they remember lands which lay waste in several districts not only of this parish, but in several parts of the island, for want of inhabitants to occupy them. Of late, the inhabitants have multiplied so much, that from August 1771 to October 1790, eight large transports have sailed from this island with emigrants, to seek settlement in America; the last of these transports sailed on the 6th of this month (October 1790) from Loch Bracadale. These 8 ships have, at a very moderate computation, carried away from this island 2400 souls, and £24,000 Sterling, ship-freights included. From the year 1772 to 1775, 204 males and 207 females emigrated from this parish to America, exclusive of those who have gone in the two last ships; yet the population appears to be as great as in 1772.

    This increase of population may be attributed to a more judicious and rational treatment of children and women in child-bed than was formerly observed; and above all, to the inoculation of the small-pox, which has been universally practised in this island for 30 years past, and has been the means of preserving many lives. The number of souls in this parish at present amounts to fully 3000. The return to Dr Webster [for an Ecclesiastical Census of Scotland], about 40 years ago, was only 2568.

Though there are no extraordinary instances of longevity, yet several in this parish arrive at a good old age. There are at present two men, one of them 88, the other 95, and two women, one of them 93, and the other 97 years. In every district of the parish, there are some weavers, male and female, a few tailors, a blacksmith in every barony, some boat-builders and house-carpenters. Every farm keeps boats, and the people go a-fishing for their own use, or when they see an appearance of herrings. There are very few bred seamen, but all [are] expert rowers, good hardy watermen, and skilled in making a boat with sails. There are 4 students from this parish who attend the Universities of Aberdeen.

There are 7 established clergymen in this island, viz. 5 on Lord Macdonald's estates, and 2 on Colonel Macleod's. All the inhabitants of Sky are Protestants, of the established Church of Scotland, a very few excepted, who are of the Church of England; yet these persons are endued with such liberality of sentiments, and so free from bigotry, that they frequent the established Church, and communicate at the Sacrament of the Lord's Supper. Marriages here produce, in general, from 5 to 12 children and upwards. The cottages are full of inhabitants.

I would have thought that ages between 88 and 97 could be described as rather more than just 'a good old age'. I wonder just how old his parishioners would have had to be, before the Revd Mr Bethune did consider them 'extraordinary instances of longevity'!

THE LANGUAGE OF THE PEOPLE

The number of people in Scotland speaking Gaelic keeps decreasing: the 2001 census shows there are only 58,650 people aged three and over who still speak the language. Although Gaelic is now confined to the Inner and Outer Hebrides and the far west of the Scottish mainland, its speakers once covered a much bigger area. Writing in the 1790s, the Revd David Dow, minister of the parish of Dron in the south of Perthshire, reported in the 'Old' Statistical Account that:

The language spoken here is Scotch, with a provincial accent or tone; the pronunciation rather slow and drawling, and apt to strike the ear of a stranger as disagreeable. The Language of all ranks, however, is improving by a more liberal education, and a more extensive intercourse with society. No Gaelic is spoken here at present, or understood by the inhabitants; but it is said to have been the common language, not only here in the neighbourhood of the Grampians but even through the whole county of Fife, not above two or three generations back.

By 1845 English had penetrated much farther north, and the Revd Hugh Mackay Mackenzie in the parish of Tongue on the west coast of Sutherland wrote that:

The language of the peasantry is Gaelic; in it they invariably converse with one another, but, owing to the influx of persons from the south, the influence of schools, and the frequency with which they go south in quest of labour, English is generally understood by the young, and spoken by many of them with considerable accuracy.

The Revd Charles Calder Mackintosh, minister of the parish of Tain on the east coast of Ross and Cromarty, compared the state of the parish in 1837 with its situation fifty years earlier, and noted 'a very striking advance in almost every department'. He observed that:

> The most important change, however, seems to be that of language. That from the peculiar situation of the Highlands of Scotland, the change is a necessary one, and that by it the avenues of knowledge are being opened up, and the power of doing good proportionally increased, may readily be allowed; but no Highlander watching the process in its immediate effects can look on it without regret.
>
> The stream of traditionary wisdom descending from our forefathers has been interrupted in its flow; the feelings and the sentiments of a race, distinguished for high feeling and noble sentiment, will not transfuse themselves into a foreign tongue; and the link of connection between the present and the past generations has been snapped. The prejudices and superstitions of the Highlander are indeed perishing along with his better characteristics; but even this will not be contemplated with unmixed satisfaction, by those who believe that there are prejudices that elevate, more than they darken the mind.
>
> Before now, the Gael was debarred from fame, because he could speak only an uncultivated, though copious and nervous tongue; now, he may chance as effectually to be debarred, because the fountain of Highland prejudice and Highland enthusiasm has been checked and rendered turbid at its source, and it may be long ere its inspiring waters renew their ancient flow. Still the change, we have said, is a necessary, and will in the end be a beneficial one; and the sooner, therefore, it be accomplished now, perhaps the better.

There are no doubt many who would take issue with the idea that Gaelic is an 'uncultivated tongue', and that its retreat in the face of English is 'a beneficial change'. To judge by his surname, however, the Revd Mr Mackintosh was himself one of those Highlanders watching with regret the eclipse of Gaelic by 'a foreign tongue'.

Although there has been a great revival of interest in things Highland since 1837, today television and the Internet have strengthened the position of the English language even more. Between 1991 and 2001, the number of Gaelic speakers decreased by 11 per cent. Unless the current rate of decline is slowed, in a hundred years time, there will be no Gaelic speakers left in Scotland at all.

SUPERSTITIONS

Some of the 'superstitions of the Highlander' alluded to by the Revd Mr Mackintosh were described by the Revd John Noble, minister of the parish of Fodderty, also in Ross and Cromarty. In the New Statistical Account he described how many 'superstitious notions' were still prevalent among 'the common people' in the 19th century:

They are firm believers in dreams and warnings – the taisg or wraith – and also in a kind of fairies or cursed spirits who resided in a small knoll directly opposite Knock-Farril; by whom children were often stolen or changed, before they were christened. Here, the old inhabitants say that even in their day, unearthly music has been heard and unearthly lights seen; but that the cursed spirits have been, long since, laid under a restraint which prevents them from making their appearance or doing mischief as formerly.

There is a small spring which rises in a circular hollow in a solid rock on the west side of Rhoagie, called Tobar-na-domhnuich, the water of which is believed to possess the virtue of indicating whether a sick person shall survive or not. It is taken from the spring before sunrise, and after the patient has been bathed or immersed in it, if the water appears of a pure colour, it foretells his recovery; but, if of a brown mossy colour, that he will die.

About six years ago, a mother brought her sickly child a distance of thirty miles, to this spring. On approaching it, she was startled by the appearance of an animal with glaring eye-balls leaping into it. The poor mother considered this as a fatal omen. Her affection for her child, however, overcame her fear. She dislodged the animal and bathed the child, after which it slept more soundly than it had ever done before. This seemed at first to confirm the sanitary virtue of the water, but the child has since died.

Within the same period, two friends of a parishioner whose life was despaired of, went to consult the spring in his behalf, and to fetch some of the water. On placing the pitcher in it, the water assumed a circular motion from south to west. They returned with joy, and informed the patient, that there was no cause to fear, as the motion of the water, being from south to west, was a sure indication that he should recover, whereas, if it had been from north to west, he should die. The person still lives.

Highlanders were not the only people described as superstitious. Also in the New Statistical Account, the Revd Alexander Spence (who contributed the section on fisheries for the city of Aberdeen) commented about the Aberdeen fishermen that:

Like most other fishermen, they have a good many superstitious ideas and practices, and they have implicit faith in many traditions and in various omens. Thus they reckon it very offensive for any one to count a boat's crew, or a company of them returning from market, and it is not less so to tell how many fish they have caught. If a fisher be turned back when he is going out to fish, he will on no account go out that day, and is very much provoked. Often too, things which any one but they would esteem mere trifles, cannot be spoken of without interfering with some omen, whose influence they would hold it sinful to doubt.

It is at the same time to be noticed, that the fishers of Futtie [a fishing village at the mouth of the River Dee, one of Aberdeen's two rivers] have less superstitions than those that live in the fishing-villages along the coast, both to the north and south, where they live almost entirely secluded from intercourse with the inland agricultural population.

It is probable that there have been fishers settled at the mouth of the Dee, both in Futtie and at Torrie [on the south side], ever since Aberdeen became a town of any noticeable magnitude. The fishers who now inhabit these villages are, like those along most of the east coast of Scotland, evidently of a race distinct from the other inhabitants, and from their aspect, features, and other circumstances, it seems probable that they have come from the opposite coasts of Denmark and Sweden.

MINISTERS' OPINIONS AND PREJUDICES

Writing accounts of their parishes gave the ministers an opportunity to ride some of their hobby-horses. The Revd Thomas Birnie, for example, writing in the 'Old' Statistical Account about the parish of Alford in Aberdeenshire, grumbled that:

> ... harvest fees have been rising for some years, and are now £1 15 shillings or £2 for a man, and £1 for a woman, besides victuals; and the risk of bad weather, to protract the harvest and lay hands idle, whom the farmer must maintain, and every thing else being taken into view, it will be found that the expence of harvest work runs very greatly out of proportion to that of every other species of labour.
>
> This disproportion is the cause of many of the grievances we feel with regard to ordinary servants; for these high harvest fees being nearly equivalent to a half year's wages, not only deter the people, especially women, from engaging to work to a master, but induces servants to desert their service upon the slightest pretences; and it is much to be regretted that the dislike of getting what they call a 'bad word' among servants generally ties up the farmer from applying for that redress which the law affords.
>
> The same silly idea leads them to give way to the grossest abuses in their domestic concerns. A farmer must often rise from bed at 3 or 4 o'clock in a winter's morning, to admit his servants, who have been junketing all night in the neighbourhood; and he must perform all the morning work of a farm, in tending cattle etc, long before they get up to assist him; nor is it uncommon for a farmer to go with his cart and horses to Aberdeen himself, because he will not only take better care of his cattle, but perform the journey at less expence than his servant. In short, the common meaning of language here is totally reversed and servants do not so much serve as rule and tyrannize over their masters.

Writing about the parish of Douglas, Lanarkshire in 1835, the minister (another Revd Alexander Stewart) complained that:

> Unfortunately for the morals of the people, there are no fewer than 12 public houses in the parish, including the two principal inns at Douglas and Douglas mill. Another circumstance very prejudicial to the morals of the people is the number of fairs, of which there are 7 in the course of the year. These the working classes keep as holidays; and as few of them think of resuming their labours till the following week, there is a great loss of time, with a most ruinous waste of means. Most of these fairs might be abolished not only without detriment, but with great advantage to the place.

The Revd Mr Stewart would no doubt be pleased to know that the fairs that he found so objectionable have now all gone, although whether he would be impressed by the morals he would find today is another matter.

Part Three

General Information

11 Records at the National Archives of Scotland

The National Archives of Scotland (NAS, formerly known as the Scottish Record Office) is one of the two major repositories of Scottish historical records, the other being the General Register Office for Scotland (GROS). The collection of testaments in the National Archives (including wills and inventories) has already been put online through the Scottish Archive Network (SCAN) (see Chapter 4), a partnership of the NAS, the Heritage Lottery Fund, and the Genealogical Society of Utah (GSU, part of the Church of Jesus Christ of Latter-day Saints).

SCAN's stated aim is to revolutionise access to Scotland's archives by providing a single online catalogue to the holdings of over 50 Scottish archives, and this work is in progress. You can find information about and also access the catalogue at www.scan.org.uk/scan2003/aboutus/indexonline.htm. Besides its testaments, the

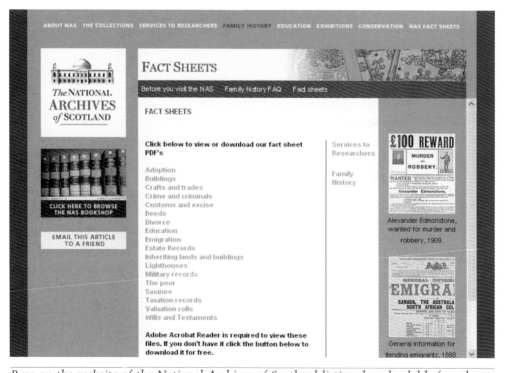

Page on the website of the National Archives of Scotland listing downloadable fact sheets.

NAS also holds many other records of interest to family historians, and SCAN is currently digitising many of the church records held by the NAS in a major project expected to take 5-7 years. In addition, the NAS is hoping to digitise its registers of sasines, poor relief registers, and taxation records.

A. CHURCH RECORDS

In 1560 the Scottish Parliament changed the country's form of Christian worship from Roman Catholic to Protestant. In particular, the Church of Scotland became presbyterian, organised on the basis of a number of courts: at parish level, the kirk session; at district level, the presbytery; and at national level, the General Assembly, which is chaired by a Moderator elected for a period of one year. There are no bishops or archbishops in the Church of Scotland, and only God is recognised as head of the church.

The Old Parish Registers (OPRs) of the Church of Scotland, containing entries recording baptisms (and sometimes also births), proclamation of banns before a marriage (and sometimes actual marriages), and burials (and sometimes deaths) are held by the GROS. Indexes to the OPRs are available online via the *ScotlandsPeople* website (see Chapter 3), and the images of the actual records are expected to be put online during 2004. The kirk session records of the Church of Scotland are mainly held by the NAS, although there is some kirk session material in the parish registers.

During the 17th century bishops were re-introduced into the Church of Scotland, and 'covenanters' who had signed the National Covenant at Greyfriars Church in Edinburgh in 1638 (to keep the freedom of the church) were persecuted. In 1689 Britain's last Roman Catholic king, James VII of Scotland (and II of England), fled after the 'Glorious Revolution'.

The Revolution Settlement which followed in 1690 restored presbyterianism to the Church of Scotland, and led to the breakaway of the Scottish Episcopal Church (a member of the Anglican family of churches). In addition, some covenanters formed the Reformed Presbyterian Church (the 'Cameronians').

Secessions from the Church of Scotland

In 1733 the Original Secession Church was formed by the Revd Ebenezer Erskine and others, who left the Church of Scotland because they were against the right of landowners to appoint ministers to the churches on their estates ('patronage'). The Secession Church then split in 1747 into 'Burghers' (the Associate Synod) and 'Anti-Burghers' (the General Associate Synod) over whether or not burgesses (city dignitaries) should take an oath acknowledging the 'true religion'.

Both the Burghers and Anti-Burghers broke into 'Auld Lichts' (Old Lights) and 'New Lichts' (New Lights), the former in 1799 and the latter in 1806. The Auld

Lichts believed the state should support the church (establishmentarianism), while the New Lichts held that church and state should be independent (disestablishmentarianism or voluntaryism).

Meanwhile, in 1761, a second secession from the Church of Scotland had taken place, again over patronage. The Revd Thomas Gillespie had been expelled from his church, and formed the Presbytery of Relief (the Relief Church) with two colleagues.

By far the biggest breakaway from the Church of Scotland occurred in 1843, however, when – in what was known as the 'Disruption' – the Revd Thomas Chalmers and over 450 other ministers (one third of the total number) left to form the Free Church of Scotland. Yet again, the dispute was over patronage, particularly in the Highlands. By 1851 there were nearly 900 Free Church congregations.

Unions of Secession Churches

This complicated picture becomes even more so, because many of the seceding churches united with others, although often the unions were not complete, with a rump of one of the churches carrying on. In 1820 the 154 congregations of New Licht Burghers and the 129 congregations of New Licht Anti-Burghers merged as the United Secession Church, while the Auld Licht Burghers rejoined the Church of Scotland in 1839, with the Auld Licht Anti-Burghers continuing as the Original Secession Church.

In 1847 all of the United Secession Church and 118 of the 136 Relief Church congregations joined together as the United Presbyterian Church, which had 465 congregations by 1851. In 1852 and 1876, respectively, the Original Secession Church and the Reformed Presbyterian Church joined the Free Church, but with minorities continuing in those churches. In 1893 some Free Church members broke away as the Free Presbyterian Church.

In 1900 the United Presbyterian Church and the Free Church joined as the United Free Church, although 25 Free Church ministers and 63 congregations remained outside this union. A major change occurred in 1929, when the United Free Church rejoined the Church of Scotland, although a minority continued in the United Free Church.

And still the splits continue, with the Associated Presbyterian Church breaking away from the Free Presbyterian Church in 1989, and the Free Church Continuing splitting from the Free Church in 2000. Scotland has rightly been called the most 'reformed' nation of the Reformation, as the above church history demonstrates. Despite the country's 400 protestant years, however, the Roman Catholic Church is again strong in Scotland, having experienced a resurgence as a result of Irish immigration in the 19th century.

Church Records at the NAS

The NAS holds many registers of the presbyterian churches that seceded from the Church of Scotland (including baptisms, marriages, burials and minutes of the kirk sessions), as well as those of some congregations of the Scottish Episcopal Church. It also holds some records of other denominations (including Roman Catholic, Congregational and Quaker records).

The NAS also holds some Church of Scotland registers that supplement, wholly or partly, the parish registers held by the GROS. (See Appendix 2.) The church records currently being digitised are those of secession church congregations that rejoined the Church of Scotland in 1909 and 1929, and whose records form part of an existing Church of Scotland congregation.

B. LAND RECORDS

Most land in Scotland is still held through the feudal system, under which all land is held in a hierarchical structure under the Crown, with no land owned outright. The person at the bottom of the chain is known as the 'vassal' (whom most people would think of as the owner of the land), while those above him or her are 'superiors'. The military service that vassals originally owed to their feudal superiors in return for the land has long been replaced by the payment of money.

One of the first acts of the new Scottish Parliament (see Chapter 13) was the enacting of land reform laws. Although the Abolition of Feudal Tenure Act 2000, through which the feudal system is being replaced by a system where land *is* owned outright, passed into law on 9 June 2002, most of its provisions will not come into force until 28 November 2004, because of the need for many transitional arrangements.

Retours (Services of Heirs)

Under the feudal system, when a vassal died his heir had to prove his right to inherit before a jury of local landowners, whose findings were written up as a 'retour' (return) to the Royal Chancery. If the retour was satisfactory, the person would be 'served as heir' (recognised as heir). The NAS holds these retours or 'services of heirs', which are in Latin until 1847, apart from between 1652 and 1659 (during the Commonwealth). Retours were used much less after 1868, after which land could be passed on via a will.

Registers of Sasines

The document that records the transfer of ownership (through sale or inheritance) of a piece of land or a building is called a sasine (pronounced 'say-zin'), which usually specifies the names of the old and new owners, together with a description of the property. The NAS, which holds the registers of sasines (except all of those for Glasgow, and those for Aberdeen and Dundee before 1809), warns that before the 20th century most Scots rented rather than owned the property they lived in, and so will not be mentioned in the registers.

The earliest register of sasines, known as the 'Secretary's Register', was started in 1599 and ran until 1609, but is very incomplete. From 1617 there were 'particular registers of sasines' for most counties and a 'general registers of sasines' based at Edinburgh for properties anywhere in Scotland except the Lothians or extending over county boundaries.

In 1869 the particular and general registers were replaced by one general register arranged in county divisions. The 66 'royal burghs' of Scotland kept their own registers of sasines. The NAS describes the registers as 'fairly complete' from 1617 and 'fully comprehensive' from around 1660.

Since 1979 the register of sasines is gradually being replaced by a Land Register, which is a plans-based system set up as a register of title (ROT) rather than a register of deeds. A once-and-for-all examination of relevant deeds is being carried out by Registers of Scotland, a government agency, and all the relevant information transferred to a Title Sheet.

Search Sheets

The NAS points out that, with the variety of indexes to the registers of sasines, you may be well advised to buy the relevant 'search sheet' for a piece of land or building. These search sheets were first produced in 1878, and specify the volume and page numbers of all the sasines and deeds for a given property.

A computerised version was created in 1993, and the old search sheets have been digitised by Registers of Scotland, which provides a web-based service called 'Registers Direct', giving access to both the register of sasines search sheets and the Land Register. This service is aimed at business customers who pay by invoice, although Registers of Scotland say family historians could use it by making an advance payment. The agency suggests, however, that it may be better to use the Search Request Form in the Citizen's Area (www.ros.gov.uk/citizen/searchform. htm), specifying 'family history' in section Q3 as the reason for the search.

Valuation Rolls

From 1854, and the passage of the Lands Valuation (Scotland) Act, until the introduction in 1989 of the Community Charge (a form of poll tax) for domestic properties, valuation rolls were compiled annually for each burgh and county in Scotland. The NAS holds all these rolls, as well as those for businesses in the years since 1988.

The valuation rolls list the name and designation of the proprietor of each property, as well as the names of the tenant, occupier, and the property's annual rateable value, but without the names of any other residents. The valuation rolls are not indexed, and for the major cities (Glasgow, Edinburgh, Aberdeen and Dundee), the rolls extend to several volumes. The entries are arranged by parish (in the counties) or electoral ward (in the cities), street, and house name or number.

C. CRIMINAL COURT RECORDS

The supreme criminal court in Scotland is the High Court of Justiciary, which deals with serious crimes, such as murder, treason, heresy, counterfeiting and sexual crimes, and also acts as an appeal court for criminal cases in sheriff courts. Most High Court cases are not indexed, although there are typescript indexes for 1611-1631 and 1699-1720. Manuscript lists of cases heard in Edinburgh and on local circuits from 1537 are available in the NAS search rooms, as are 'Books of Adjournal', which record the sittings in Edinburgh from 1576, stating indictments and giving a brief record of proceedings in the court. There are also minute books recording the court proceedings, verdict and sentence.

Few of the precognitions (written reports of the evidence of witnesses to a crime) from the Lord Advocate's Department have survived from earlier than 1812. There is

Web page showing the results of a search in the online catalogue of the National Archives of Scotland.

a card index for the years up to 1900, however, which refers to a detailed catalogue giving name, occupation, residence, and the alleged crime. In addition, records are available of cases before a jury in the sheriff courts, which dealt with theft and assault cases.

Prison Registers

Prison registers are also held by the NAS, although most of these are unindexed. In the Home and Health Department papers there are registers for Edinburgh (Calton) Prison and Bridewell (1798-1874), Glasgow Duke Street and Barlinnie (1841-1966), Aberdeen (1809-1960), and Perth (1867-1961), and for other smaller prisons. In the Sheriff Court records are prison registers for Angus (1805-1827), Ayr (1860-1863), Fort William (1893-1936), Jedburgh (1839-1893), Kirkcudbright (1791-1811), Selkirk (1828-1840) and Stirling (1822-1829). Prison registers are closed for 75 years after the date of the last entry.

Covenanters and other people banished to the North American colonies in the 17th century are listed in the Registers of the Privy Council, which have been published for 1545-1691, with a comprehensive index. Those who took part in the Jacobite uprisings in 1715 and 1745 were tried in England, and records are held in The National Archives in London. The NAS does hold some records of Jacobite treason trials in 1748-49, however, as well as certificates for convicts transported to North America in the 1770s.

D. TAXATION RECORDS

Up to the 17th century, taxation fell on landowners, taxes being raised for specific purposes, such as defence or the king's marriage. In the 1690s the Scottish Parliament put a tax of 14 shillings on every hearth in Scotland to raise money for the Army. The hearth tax was payable by landowners and tenants, the only exceptions being hospitals and the poor.

The NAS holds hearth lists for most of Scotland, although there are none for any parishes in Caithness or Orkney. Most of the lists are in county and parish order, with the number of hearths in the parish, the names of the owners or tenants of houses, and the number and names of the poor who were exempt from the tax, but some hearth lists contain less information. The list for Glasgow, for example, states only the total number of hearths and the amount of money collected, while that for Inverness-shire lists the total number of hearths, headed by the name of the owner and the names of individual paupers.

In 1694, 1695 and 1698 (twice) poll taxes (i.e. payable by each individual person) were levied to pay off the debts and arrears of the Army and Navy, with payment graduated at the rate of six shillings and upwards according to rank and means, the only exemptions being the poor and children under 16 years of age. The NAS holds a number of poll tax lists, although for many counties there are lists for only one or two parishes.

Various other taxes were levied after 1748, including:

- Window Tax (1747/8-1798);
- Commutation Tax (1784-1798);
- Inhabited House Tax (1778-1798);
- Shop Tax (1785-1789);
- Male Servants' Tax (1777-1798);
- Female Servants' Tax (1785-1792);
- Cart Tax (1785-1798);
- Carriage Tax (1785-1798);
- Horse Tax (1785-1798);
- Farm Horse Tax (1797-1798);
- Dog Tax (1797-1798);
- Clock and Watch Tax (1797-1798);
- Aid and Contribution Tax (1797-1798);
- Income Tax (1799-1802);
- Consolidated Schedules of Assessed Taxes (1798-1799).

E. POOR RELIEF RECORDS

Before the passing of the Poor Law Amendment (Scotland) Act in 1845, providing benefit for the poorer members of society was the joint responsibility of local landowners (heritors) and kirk sessions. Information on poor relief can be found in the NAS's holdings of heritor and kirk session records, although lists of distributions to the poor can be difficult to locate, as these are not usually recorded separately.

In 1845 parochial boards were formed for the administration of poor relief, which were required to maintain a list of those receiving relief, with details of each person's name, age, country and place of birth, and marital status, as well as information about a man's wife and children. Although the NAS holds parochial board records for some parishes in East Lothian, Midlothian and Wigtownshire, most of these records are held in local archives.

The NAS also holds records relating to poor relief provided through private charities, such as:

- The King James VI Hospital, Perth;

- The Dean Orphanage, Edinburgh;

- Dr Guthrie's Schools, Edinburgh;

- George Heriot's School, Edinburgh;

- Trinity House, Leith.

F. ADOPTION RECORDS

The NAS holds no adoption records from before the passing of the Adoption of Children (Scotland) Act in 1930, which introduced legal adoption in Scotland. Before that time adoptions had been privately arranged by individual people or charitable adoption agencies. Since 1930 adoptions arranged by charities or local government social services departments have been ratified in the sheriff courts, with a small number going through the Court of Session in Edinburgh. The records are held by the court for 25 years, after which they are transferred to the NAS.

Adoption records are extremely confidential, usually containing a copy of the adopted person's original birth certificate together with a report to the court and other papers. The adoption records are sealed and closed to even NAS staff, and will not be open to general public access until the records are 100 years old, i.e. from 2030 onwards. The adopted person him- or herself is allowed to see the records, once he or she reaches 16 years of age, as well as a person authorised by him or her. It's very rare for anyone else to be allowed to see the records, even after the adopted person has died. This can make things very difficult for family historians who want to see the adoption papers of a parent or grandparent who is deceased.

G. OTHER RECORDS AT THE NAS

In addition to the various types of record mentioned above, the NAS also holds civil court records (including those of divorces), registers of deeds (including bonds, tacks (leases), apprenticeship records, marriage contracts, and some wills), various landed estate papers, Customs & Excise records (including shipping registers and some staff records), craft and trade records, militia lists, and records of lighthouses and their keepers.

H. FURTHER INFORMATION

More information on most of the records held by the NAS is contained in a series of factsheets, which can be downloaded as 'pdf' (Portable Document Format) files from the NAS website at www.nas.gov.uk/family_history.htm. The factsheets give the general reference numbers for the collections held by the NAS, such as 'CH2' for Church of Scotland kirk session records.

The reference number together with a placename can then be used to search the NAS online public catalogue at 195.153.34.3.dservea/ for the catalogue entries for kirk session records for a particular parish. Entering 'CH2' and 'Arbroath' brings up a list of 12 kirk session catalogue entries, such as:

CH2/1400   **Arbroath**, St Margaret's Kirk Session   1875-1960

12 Scottish Heraldry and the Records of the Lyon Court

INTRODUCTION

The Lord Lyon King of Arms is responsible for everything to do with heraldry and coats of arms in Scotland. Not only is the Lord Lyon a government minister, he's also a judge, who sits in court in a robe of crimson velvet and ermine. The Court of the Lord Lyon (in New Register House in Edinburgh, which also houses the General Register Office for Scotland (GROS)) both establishes and protects individuals' and companies' rights to coats of arms. The Lyon Court has a website at www.lyon-court.com.

As well as the Lord Lyon, there are ten other Scottish Officers of Arms with wonderful titles, such as the Albany, Rothesay, and Ross Heralds, and the Unicorn, Carrick, and Bute Pursuivants. The Heralds are senior and the Pursuivants junior members of the Royal Household. Other Officers of Arms are the Orkney Herald Extraordinary and the Linlithgow Pursuivant Extraordinary, as well as the Lyon Court's Procurator Fiscal (its public prosecutor) and the Herald Painter.

Heraldry began about 1,000 years ago, both through the designs used on personal seals to identify the person who had signed a document (in an age when few could read or write), and also so that knights wearing full body armour and a helmet could be identified. The medieval-style tabard, a jacket which the knight wore over his armour, is still worn today by the Lyon Court's Officers of Arms. This is the origin of the expression 'coat of arms', although nowadays the term applies to the design on it, rather than the tabard itself.

The Officers of Arms take part in a number of state ceremonies each year, in which they wear their tabards, which display the Royal Arms. These ceremonies include the opening of the General Assembly of the Church of Scotland in May, and the General Assembly service at St Giles' Cathedral (the High Kirk of Edinburgh).

Other ceremonies that the Officers of Arms take part in include the annual commemoration service at the Scottish National War Memorial in Edinburgh Castle in June, and the St Andrew's Day service at St Giles' Cathedral in November, as well as occasional ceremonies including the installation service for a Knight of the Thistle, the installation of the Governor of Edinburgh Castle, and any proclamations.

You can find more information on Scottish Heraldry and the Officers of the Lyon Court at the website of the Heraldry Society of Scotland (www.heraldry-scotland.co.uk). Clicking on the link to 'Scottish Heraldry' brings up a page with the colourful heraldic shields of 15 ancient earldoms of Scotland, together with links to interesting articles on heraldic topics.

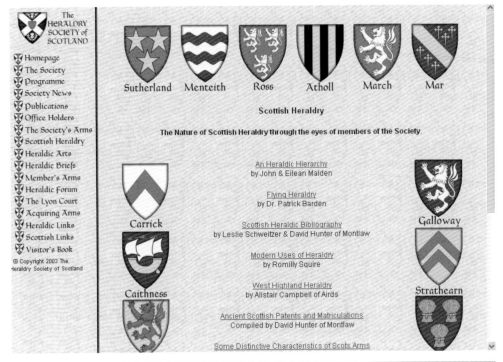

Page from the website of the Heraldry Society of Scotland, showing the shields of some of the ancient Scottish earldoms.

HISTORY OF THE LYON COURT AND ITS GENEALOGICAL RECORDS

The first time the office of Lord Lyon was mentioned in records was in 1318, when an appointment to the position was made by King Robert I of Scotland (Robert the Bruce), and the names are known of all the office-holders since 1388. The post of Lord Lyon derives from that of the ancient High Sennachie, who verified the ancestry of the King of Scotland and crowned him at his coronation. The importance of the Lord Lyon is indicated by his use of the royal coat of arms, and his title comes from the use of the lion rampant in the Scottish royal arms.

Since 1592 the Lord Lyon has been responsible for prosecuting anyone using a coat of arms that is not his to use. This is a criminal offence in Scotland. Although the maximum fine for using unauthorised arms is only £100, the Lord Lyon can insist that they're removed from buildings and that any flags incorporating the arms are taken down.

In 1672 a 'Public Register of All Arms and Bearings in Scotland' was created by an Act of the Scottish Parliament. This register, known as the Lyon Register, was established as a central record of all the coats of arms authorised by the Lord Lyon. For the first five years registration was free of charge to encourage those already using arms to register them.

The Lyon Register is still in use, as is the 'Public Register of Genealogies and Birthbrieves in Scotland', both of which contain genealogical information about Scottish families. Most of this is in the Lyon Register, however, which is being digitised, and will be accessible via the Internet by about 2006 or 2007. This will be part of a new 'Scottish Family History Service', which will bring together the online services of the GROS, the National Archives of Scotland (NAS), and the Court of the Lord Lyon.

COATS OF ARMS, CLANS AND TARTANS

The Lord Lyon is at pains to point out that a coat of arms belongs to only one person at a time: there's no such thing as a clan or family coat of arms. A clan chief has a coat of arms that's personal to him or her, and which no-one else is allowed to use, despite the impression you may be given by people who want to sell you a coat of arms for your clan or family. If you *are* a member of a clan, you're allowed to wear the chief's crest (the figure that sits on top of the helmet above the shield in the coat of arms) encircled by a strap and buckle containing his motto.

If you've a clan surname you can find out who your chief is by checking the list of 'Chiefs of Clans and Names' at www.electricscotland.com/webclans/chiefs.htm. You'll see (for example) that Hamish Chisholm of Chisholm is The Chisholm (as the chief of Clan Chisholm is known), the Duke of Argyll is chief of the Campbells, the Earl of Cromartie chief of the MacKenzies, and Madam Jean Moffat of that Ilk head of the Moffats.

As far as tartan is concerned, you may wear the tartan of your clan, but the Lord Lyon points out that you don't have the right to wear your mother's tartan unless you've taken her surname. If you don't have a clan surname you may wear a district tartan (such as Lennox, Huntly or Strathearn) if you have an ancestor who lived in that district. Otherwise you may wear the Jacobite, Caledonia, Black Watch or Hunting Stewart tartan.

Applying for a Coat of Arms
If you want to use a coat of arms yourself, you can apply to the Lord Lyon for a Grant of Arms, which can be made to any 'virtuous and well-deserving person'

who either owns property in Scotland or has Scottish ancestry. When your arms are granted, you get an illuminated parchment with the coat of arms painted by a heraldic artist and the text stating your pedigree written by a calligrapher. The arms are also recorded in the Lyon Register.

If you can prove that one of your ancestors had a coat of arms, then instead of applying for new arms you can 'matriculate' arms (based on the existing coat), which costs about half as much as a grant of new arms (see Appendix 1). Even new arms are designed to look similar to the existing arms of people of the same name, so that you can identify with the family. In my own case, if I were to apply for a coat of arms the Lord Lyon might come up with arms similar to those of the Earl of Galloway, who's the head of the senior branch of the Stewart family, or perhaps something like the arms of Andrew Stewart, the 17th Chief of Clan Stewart of Appin (see the section on clans in the following chapter).

Flags

The Lord Lyon has authority to rule on the use of heraldic flags in Scotland. He also points out that, while flying the union flag (better known as the 'union jack') and/or the saltire (the St Andrew's cross) is correct for Scots, use of the royal standard (with the rampant lion) by ordinary people is illegal. Just don't tell the Scottish football supporters!

13 The Scottish People: History, Clans and Names

INTRODUCTION

Although Scotland shares the same island with England and Wales, the Scots certainly don't consider themselves to be English. British, yes. English, definitely not. To people living elsewhere, this can seem strange. After all, the Scots speak the same language as the English, don't they? Setting Gaelic aside for the moment, there are those who'll argue that (broad) Scots is a separate language from English. Ah weel, ah dinnae ken aboot that.

Since 1 July 1999 Scotland has had its own parliament, which sits in Edinburgh and has certain powers and responsibilities devolved to it by the UK Parliament in London. You can watch the 129 Members of the Scottish Parliament (MSPs) debating 'live' in the Main Chamber and sitting in parliamentary committees via the Scottish Parliament website (www.scottish.parliament.uk). The government of Scotland is known as the Scottish Executive, a name that also covers the Scottish civil service departments.

Scotland is not an independent country, however: it's still part of the United Kingdom of Great Britain and Northern Ireland. Before 1707 Scotland *was* completely independent, although in 1603 King James VI of Scotland became James I of England as well, and moved to London. The present Scottish Parliament is responsible for agriculture, education, health and justice and can pass laws on these matters.

Even before 1999 Scotland was different to England and Wales in many respects: it had (and still has) its own legal system, banking system (with its own bank notes), local government system, national church (the Church of Scotland, whose Earthly head is the 'Moderator of the General Assembly' chosen annually from among its ministers), education system, its own kinds of beer ('light' and 'heavy', rather than the 'mild' and 'bitter' of England, although 'export' is preferred by many), and of course, its own civil registration system.

SCOTTISH HISTORY FROM A GENEALOGICAL VIEWPOINT

*c.*3,000-2,000 BC	Mesolithic (middle-stone-age) hunters and fishermen arrive in what is now called Scotland, probably via a land bridge from the Continent.
*c.*2,000 BC	Arrival of Neolithic (new-stone-age) farmers from the Continent.

c.1,800 BC	Arrival of the so-called 'beaker people', late Neolithic/Early Bronze-Age warriors, probably originally from Spain.
c.700 BC onwards	Settlement of the Brythonic (Old Welsh-speaking) Celts. Later these and the earlier peoples are known as the 'Picts'.
78 AD	Invasion of (what is now) southern Scotland by the Romans, led by Gnaeus Julius Agricola.
84	Battle of Mons Graupius. The Romans (under Agricola) defeat the Picts (under Calgacus).
85	The Romans build forts between the Clyde and the Forth. People the Romans call the Caledonii are to the north, and the Maetae to the south.
122-128	The Roman Emperor Hadrian has a 73-mile stone wall built across the north of (what later becomes) England to keep the Picts out of the Roman province of Britannia.
142	The Roman Emperor Antoninus Pius has a 36-mile turf wall built, joining up the line of forts in the Forth-Clyde valley. The south of modern Scotland is a Roman military zone.
c.500	The Gaelic-speaking Scots from Ireland begin to settle in Argyll.
547	The Angles conquer Lothian, which becomes part of their kingdom of Northumbria.
c.794	Start of attacks by Norse Vikings.
843	Picts and Scots united under King Kenneth MacAlpin as Alba: the beginning of Scotland.
872	Orkney becomes a Norse earldom.
890	Shetland, the Hebrides and Caithness taken by the Norse.
975	Lothian comes under Scottish rule (from the Angles).
987	Sutherland, Ross and Moray taken by the Norse.
1034	Strathclyde comes under Scottish rule (from the Britons).
1134	Moray comes under Scottish rule (from the Norse).
1164	Somerled, the first real 'Lord of the Isles', is killed in battle near Renfrew.
1171	First mention of Jews in Scotland.
1196	The north of the mainland comes under Scottish rule (from the Norse).
1266	The Hebrides ceded to Scotland by the Norse.
1314	Battle of Bannockburn. The Scots (under King Robert the Bruce) defeat the English (under King Edward II).
1318	Lord Lyon King of Arms first mentioned.
1320	The Declaration of Arbroath asserts Scotland's independence from England.

1349	'The Black Death' (bubonic plague) reaches Scotland, killing about a third of the population.
1371	Accession of King Robert II, the first Stewart monarch.
1468	Orkney becomes part of Scotland (from the Norse), as part of the marriage settlement of Queen Margaret of Scotland (the 'Maid of Norway').
1469	Shetland added to Queen Margaret's marriage settlement.
1513	Battle of Flodden. The English (under Henry VIII's lieutenant Thomas Howard, Earl of Surrey) defeat the Scots (under King James IV, who is killed, along with 10,000 of his army).
1553	First entries are written in the oldest Scottish parish register in Errol in Perthshire.
1560	The Scottish Parliament declares the Church of Scotland to be Protestant, instead of Roman Catholic.
1600	The year begins on 1 January instead of 25 March.
1603	The Union of the Crowns: Scotland's King James VI becomes James I of England too.
1603-1617	First proscriptions of the MacGregors.
1633	Further proscription of the MacGregors.
1661	Proscription of the MacGregors lifted.
1662	Acts of Scottish Parliament against use of Gaelic.
1672	Lyon Register of arms established in the Court of the Lord Lyon.
1690	Revd Robert Kirk translates the Bible into Gaelic.
1690	The Episcopal Church breaks away from the Church of Scotland.
1693	The MacGregors proscribed again.
1707	The Union of the Parliaments: Scotland united with England and Wales.
1715	First major Jacobite rebellion in support of 'James VIII' (the Old Pretender).
1733	First secession from the Church of Scotland: the Original Secession Church.
1745	Second major Jacobite rebellion: 'Bonnie Prince Charlie' lands in Scotland to claim the throne for his father, 'James VIII'. The defeat of the Prince's troops at Culloden in 1746 leads to the end of the clan system and the proscription of Highland dress.
1750-1850	The 'Highland Clearances'.
1750	Norn language (a form of Norwegian) becomes extinct in Shetland.
1752	Scotland (with the rest of the UK) moves to the Gregorian calendar.
1755	Ecclesiastical census of Scotland organised by the Revd Alexander Webster. Population is estimated at 1,265,380.

1761   Second secession from the Church of Scotland: the Relief Church.

1774   Register House (home of National Archives of Scotland) built in Edinburgh's 'New Town', designed by Robert Adam.

1782   Highland dress allowed once more, and the proscription of the MacGregors lifted.

1791   Publication of first volume of *Statistical Account of Scotland*.

1801   First official census of Scotland (and the rest of the UK). Population is 1,608,420.

1834   Publication of first volume of *New Statistical Account of Scotland*.

1843   Third secession from the Church of Scotland (the 'Disruption'): the Free Church.

1855   Civil registration of births, marriages and deaths begins in Scotland.

1901   Census shows Gaelic-speaking population of Scotland to be 230,806 (out of a total population of 4,472,103).

1951   Publication of first volume of *Third Statistical Account of Scotland*.

1975   Re-organisation of Scottish local government: the 33 historic counties are replaced by 12 regions.

1996   Re-organisation of Scottish local government again: the 12 regions are replaced by 32 unitary authorities.

1998   The General Register Office for Scotland puts the indexes of Scottish births/baptisms, marriages/banns and deaths/burials (1553-1897) on-line at *Scots Origins*. These indexes are now at *ScotlandsPeople*.

1999   After nearly 300 years, Scotland again has its own parliament.

2001   Census shows Gaelic-speaking population of Scotland to be 58,650 (out of a total population of 5,062,011).

2002   Images of Scottish statutory birth and death records are made available on the new *ScotlandsPeople* website. Marriages are added in 2003.

THE SCOTTISH PEOPLE

In Roman times modern Scotland was inhabited by 16 tribes, according to the 'Geography' of Ptolemy (the ethnic Greek geographer from Alexandria in Egypt), who lived in the second century AD. These were the:

1. Caereni (in the west of Sutherland);
2. Caledonii (in the south of Perthshire);
3. Carnonacae (in Wester Ross);
4. Cornovii (in Caithness);
5. Creones (in the part of Argyll north of Loch Linnhe);
6. Decantae (in Easter Ross and Cromarty);
7. Dumnonii (in the north of Ayrshire and in Renfrewshire);

8.   Epidii (on Kintyre);
9.   Lugi (in the east of Sutherland);
10. Novantae (in Galloway);
11. Selgovae (in the counties of Peebles, Selkirk and Roxburgh);
12. Smertae (in the north of Ross and Cromarty and the south of Sutherland);
13. Taexali (in Aberdeenshire);
14. Vacomagi (in Angus);
15. Venicones (from Stirlingshire to Fife);
16. Votadini (in Lothian and Berwickshire);

The four tribes south of the Antonine Wall (the Votadini, Selgovae, Novantae and Dumnonii) were later considered to be Britons, like those living in what became England and Wales. Those to the north were the Picts, the capital of whose northern kingdom was Inverness. The southern Picts' capital was Scone, where, later, Scottish kings were crowned on the 'Stone of Destiny'.

In the sixth century AD the Scots came over from Ireland and began to settle in the west of the Pictish area, while the Angles conquered the British area of Lothian. At the end of the eighth century the Norse Vikings began attacking Scotland, particularly the north and the islands, which gradually came under Norwegian rule over the next 200 years.

The northern mainland of Scotland, together with the Hebrides, belonged to Norway for nearly 400 years. Orkney and Shetland remained Norse for almost 600 years, and their people spoke the Norn language, a form of Old Norse, until the 18th century.

The modern Scots are principally descended from those five peoples: the Angles, Britons, Norse, Picts (who included the earlier pre-Celtic settlers) and Scots. Other peoples arrived later: Normans, Flemings, a few Bretons (including the ancestors of the Stewarts), Irish (in very large numbers in the 19th century), and in the 20th century, Italians, Jews, West Indians and Asians.

CLANS

In the Highlands and the Hebrides the tribes broke up into smaller family groupings or 'clans' (from the Gaelic word for children), such as the Campbells, Stewarts, Munros, Rosses, Robertsons, and the many 'Macs' and 'Mcs' (sons of), such as the MacDonalds, MacKenzies, MacLeods and Mackintoshes ('sons of the chief'). If you look in the various books on clans and tartans, you'll find that the descent of the clan chiefs is known and documented.

Beware, however. The Stewart chiefs (including the Royal Stuarts) are descended from 'dapifers' (stewards) who lived in Dol in Brittany 950 years ago and went over to England with the Normans in 1066, and then on to Scotland, where they became

Lord High Stewards of Scotland (hence the surname). It's very tempting to believe that, because I'm a Stewart, I must be descended from those early Stewarts too.

Maybe I am. I don't know. I've been able to trace that line back to my 3x great-grandfather Alexander Stewart, who was born in Skye around 1778. The Skye parish registers don't start until the 1800s, so it's difficult to take the line any further back. Apparently, the ancestor of the Stewarts in Skye is said to have been one of the Appin branch of the Stewarts, a weaver who eloped with the chief's daughter.

That may be the case, but I can't tell whether my Alexander, who was also a weaver, was one of that earlier Stewart weaver's descendants. For all I know, Alexander's father might have changed his surname from McNab or Smith or something else to Stewart. Perhaps when DNA testing is more advanced (see Chapter 15), I may be able to tell.

There are many cases of families changing their surname to that of a clan chief whose protection they wanted. In *The Surnames of Scotland*, George F. Black writes that many people living in Argyll took on the name Campbell, those in the Western Isles and Kintyre the name Macdonald, in the northwest Mackenzie, and in Strathbogie in Aberdeenshire the name Gordon. Dr Black also mentions the 'Frasers of the boll of meal', who were originally Bissetts, and the 'Cumins of the hen-trough', who had been 'baptised' there with their new name.

In other cases, the protected family kept its own name, but was considered a 'sept' (associated family) of the clan. These sept names are the ones you'll find on lists in tartan shops, where they ask 'Is your name here?', and tell you what tartan you should wear. The tartans in use today are almost all post-1782, which is when tartan was allowed to be worn again, after it had been proscribed following the 1745-6 Jacobite rebellion. By this time, people seem to have forgotten which tartan belonged to which clan (if they were ever so specific anyway), and kilt-makers simply invented a connection.

Up to the 18th century in the Highlands (and into the 19th in Shetland), there was widespread use of patronymics, rather than surnames. So as the son of William Stewart, I would have been Alan Williamson (or McWilliam), my father would have been William Ralphson, and my grandfather Ralph Williamson (he was actually Ralph Stewart, son of William Stewart).

SCOTTISH SURNAMES

Just over an eighth of Scottish surnames begin with 'Mac' or 'Mc'. This was one of the findings of a survey carried out by Neil Bowie and G.W.L. Jackson and published on the Web in February 2003 by the General Register Office for Scotland (GROS) (www.gro-scotland.gov.uk/grosweb/grosweb.nsf/pages/01surnames). The survey ('Surnames in Scotland over the last 140 years') found that, on a national basis, there had been little change over that period.

The most common surnames in Scotland were collated from birth and death registrations that took place between 1999 and 2001. The top twenty names were:

1.	Smith	11.	Reid
2.	Brown	12.	Murray
3.	Wilson	13.	Taylor
4.	Campbell	14.	Clark
5.	Stewart	15.	Ross
6.	Thomson	16.	Watson
7.	Robertson	17.	Morrison
8.	Anderson	18.	Paterson
9.	MacDonald	19.	Young
10.	Scott	20.	Mitchell

Different spellings were counted as different names, including 'Mac' and 'Mc' names. If this had not been done, then MacDonald and McDonald counted together would have been the second most common name. Likewise, MacKenzie and McKenzie would have appeared in 12th position.

Although 'Mac' names are often thought of as Scottish, and those with the prefix 'Mc' as Irish, the survey showed that there were over three times as many Scottish surnames beginning with 'Mc' as there were with 'Mac'.

SCOTTISH FORENAMES

There may have been little change in surnames, but that has certainly not been the case with forenames, particularly those that have been given to girls. A survey of birth registrations between 1900 and 2000 was carried out by G.W.L. Jackson and G.L. Donnelly, and published on the Web by the GROS in January 2001 under the title 'Popular Forenames in Scotland, 1900-2000' at www.gro-scotland.gov. uk/grosweb/grosweb.nsf/pages/name00. A further survey of 'Popular Forenames in Scotland 2003' was published on the Web by the GROS in January 2004 at www. gro-scotland.gov.uk/grosweb/grosweb.nsf/pages/03name.

The top ten forenames given to girls in 1900 and 2003 were:

	1900		**2003**
1.	Mary	1.	Emma
2.	Margaret	2.	Ellie
3.	Elizabeth	3.	Amy
4.	Annie	4.	Sophie
5.	Jane	5.	Chloe
6.	Agnes	6.	Erin

7.	Isabella	7.	Rachel
8.	Catherine	8.	Lucy
9.	Janet	9.	Lauren
10.	Helen	10.	Katie

The survey showed that not only was none of the top ten girls' names of 1900 still in the top ten by 2003, only two were in the top 100 (Catherine at 86, and Elizabeth at 81=). The name Anna was at 25, however, and Molly, a pet name for Mary, at 27.

The top ten boys' forenames were:

1900		**2003**	
1.	John	1.	Lewis
2.	James	2.	Jack
3.	William	3.	Cameron
4.	Robert	4.	James
5.	Alexander	5.	Kyle
6.	George	6.	Ryan
7.	Thomas	7.	Ben
8.	David	8.	Callum
9.	Andrew	9.	Matthew
10.	Charles	=10.	Jamie
		=10.	Adam

Although James is the only boy's name from the 1900 top ten still in the top ten in 2003, Jack is a pet form of John (now at 24=). If James and Jamie had been counted as one name, it would have headed the list. The other boys' names from the 1900 top ten are all still in the top 100, apart from Charles.

SCOTTISH NAMING PATTERN

In the past, a naming pattern was followed in Scotland, where the first three sons were named after:
1. the paternal grandfather;
2. the maternal grandfather;
3. the father.

Correspondingly, the first three girls were named after:
1. the maternal grandmother;
2. the paternal grandmother;
3. the mother.

This is helpful when you're looking for the children of a marriage, but although this pattern was followed quite strictly (more so than in England and Wales) until about the middle of the 20th century, you can't rely on it always being used absolutely rigidly. That means that you can't simply use the names of the first two male and female children to determine the names of the grandparents.

An illegitimate child is unlikely to be named after the reputed father's family, and the same applies later on to that child's children. Also, if a grandparent had already died, the parents might not use his or her name. In addition, if the two grandparents and the father or mother all had the same common forename, that would rather tend to mess things up. And sometimes parents just pleased themselves with names for their children – just as they do today.

14 Scottish Family History Societies

SCOTTISH GENEALOGY SOCIETY

In 1953 the Scottish Genealogy Society (SGS) was founded in Edinburgh 'to promote research into Scottish family history and to advance and encourage the collection, exchange and publication of material relating to Scottish genealogy and family history.' The following year, the society began to issue a quarterly journal, *The Scottish Genealogist*.

The SGS was the first society in Scotland dedicated to genealogy, and has, from its beginnings, collected family history books, manuscripts and pedigrees in a constantly expanding library. This is housed within the society's own premises in Edinburgh (see Appendix 5), and is open to members and non-members. The library also contains an extensive microfilm and microfiche collection of Old Parish Registers and census returns, and many indexes and other information on CD-ROM.

The society has issued several genealogical publications, including *A Dictionary of Emigrant Scots* (begun by the late Donald J. Macdonald and continued by Donald Whyte, with volumes for the United States and Canada), *Perthshire Hearth Tax* (of the 1690s), and *The Naming and Numbering of Scottish Regiments of Foot, Cavalry and Militia*. In addition, the SGS pioneered recording and publishing monumental inscriptions in Scottish churchyards.

SCOTTISH FAMILY HISTORY SOCIETIES

Towards the end of the 1970s, as family history became a popular pastime, local societies were set up in Scotland's other major cities. In 1977 the Glasgow & West of Scotland Family History Society (FHS) was founded, and in the following year, the Aberdeen & North East Scotland FHS. Two years after that, the Tay Valley FHS came into being, based in Dundee.

These are large societies, which operate resource centres in their own premises, as does the Dumfries & Galloway FHS in the town of Dumfries. A further 15 local family history societies have been set up in Scotland, from Shetland to the Borders. (See Appendix 5.) Many of these societies have family history libraries, which are located in public or school libraries, or in museums. All of them are hard at work recording monumental inscriptions (MIs), indexing census returns, or transcribing

ABERDEEN & N.E. SCOTLAND FAMILY HISTORY SOCIETY

Research Centre & Shop

 Return to Society Home Page

Our Research Centre is at 158-164 King St. Aberdeen.
The opening hours are:

Monday - Friday 10.00am - 4.00pm
Tuesday & Friday 7.00pm - 10.00pm
Saturday 9.00am - 1.00pm

Our Research Centre, opened in 1987 and the first of its
kind in the country, is available for members use. The
Research Centre is the hub of the Society's activities, staffed
by volunteer members who are delighted to assist you trace
your family tree and tell you how to go about it. Facilities
include a large library, microfilm and microfiche of the IGI
(the whole world), OPR's and census records for a wide area. Research assistance into N.E. Scotland ancestry can be carried
out for out-of-area members by Society volunteers, at a nominal charge plus expenses (such as Registrar's fees, postage,
phocopies etc.). See our current scale of charges for details. For a research request (members only) please complete our
research form.

In addition to our own series of publications, a comprehensive range of publications is stocked, including those of other Scottish
Societies and the Federation of Family History Societies.

*Page on the website of the Aberdeen & North East Scotland Family History Society
describing its research centre and shop.*

other local records (and sometimes doing all three activities), which they then publish for the benefit of a wider public.

SCOTTISH ASSOCIATION OF FAMILY HISTORY SOCIETIES

In 1986 the existing societies formed the Scottish Association of Family History
Societies (SAFHS) as an umbrella group to ease communication between individual
societies. The association's main aims are 'to promote and encourage the study
of Scottish family history, and provide a forum for the exchange, collection and
distribution of information among members.' SAFHS has also issued a number of
publications, and now has 26 full-member societies (mainly in Scotland itself).

SCOTTISH FAMILY HISTORY SOCIETIES AND INTEREST GROUPS
AROUND THE WORLD

Because of the wide spread of people of Scots descent around the world, there are 17
family history societies outside Scotland that are associate members of SAFHS. Ten
of these are in Australia, three in the US, two in Canada, one in New Zealand, and

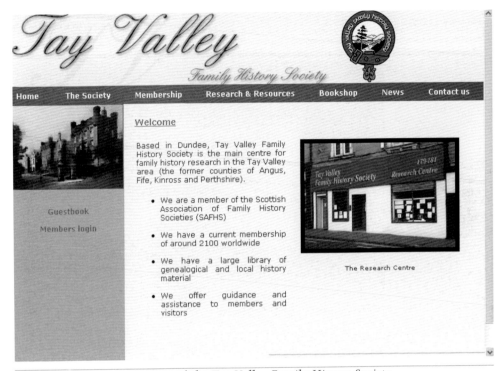

Home page of the *Tay Valley Family History Society.*

BENEFITS OF MEMBERSHIP OF A FAMILY HISTORY SOCIETY

So why would you want to join a family history society? If you live locally, you can attend society meetings, which are usually talks given by people who are experienced in family history or related matters. You can also carry out your research using the microfilms, microfiche and CD-ROMs in the FHS's research centre or library. These activities are particularly helpful, if at least some of your ancestors come from the area you live in.

If they don't, however, you'll still be able to meet and talk to fellow family historians about your shared interest, which is always good. I'm a member of the Bedfordshire FHS, although I have no ancestors from the area (as far as I know), and I go along to meetings with my wife, whose ancestors don't come from Bedfordshire either. We enjoy the talks, however, and borrow other societies' journals from the library.

It can also be a good idea to join some of the societies for the areas that your ancestors came from, as you'll find news and articles in the journals that all the

one in England. (See Appendix 5.) Several of these societies are dedicated to tracing ancestry in the British Isles, or are sub-groups with a special interest in Scotland.

Home page of the Dumfries and Galloway Family History Society showing its research centre.

FHSs publish, which can be very useful in your researches. In addition, as a member of an FHS, you can get the surnames you're interested in listed in the 'Members' Interests' published in the FHS journal. Members researching the same names can then make contact, so you may discover some fourth- or fifth-cousins, if you're lucky. You may also want to buy some of the societies' publications, such as MI listings, census indexes, and parish maps.

15 The Future of Family History: DNA

INTRODUCTION

Until fairly recently, tracing your ancestry back to about the late 1700s was about par for the course, with some fortunate people able to take their lines even further back. If you were very lucky indeed – or had chosen the right parents – you might be able to link into some well-documented family of a clan chief, the aristocracy, or even royalty.

This last is not as unlikely in Scotland as you may think. The great genealogical and heraldic writer Sir Iain Moncreiffe of that Ilk (i.e. Moncreiffe of the place also called Moncreiffe) pointed out in his introduction to *Debrett's Family Historian* (1981) that there was a strong likelihood of any Mackay clansman in Strathnaver in Sutherland descending from King Robert II of Scotland, who reigned in the 14th century.

This was because of the marriage of the king's daughter to the Macdonald Lord of the Isles, and the marriage of their daughter to the chief of the Mackays, followed by hundreds of years of local intermarriage down through the various levels of society that existed then. In the same way, wrote Sir Iain, any given Robertson in Atholl in Perthshire was likely to descend from Robert II also, as a result of the marriage of another of his daughters to the thane of Glamis, a female descendant of whom married the chief of the Robertsons in the following century.

Ian Grimble, in his book *Clans and Chiefs*, quotes General Sir David Stewart of Garth, who noted in 1822 that there were then living in Atholl upwards of 4,000 people (including nearly 2,000 with the surname Stewart) who were descendants of the illegitimate children of Robert II's son Alexander Stewart, Earl of Buchan and Badenoch (known as the 'Wolf of Badenoch' because of his wild and warlike behaviour, including the destruction of Elgin Cathedral in 1390). Robert II was the grandson of Robert I (Robert the Bruce, who lived between 1274 and 1329), who was in turn descended from King Alfred the Great of England (who was born in 849 and died in 899).

Suppose, however, that there was a way we could tell if we were descended from historical figures like Robert the Bruce or Alfred the Great without having all the paperwork to prove it. What if we could even trace our ancestors back thousands and even tens of thousands of years? Wouldn't that be wonderful? The 'magic ingredient' that's being hailed today as a great breakthrough is DNA, which *can* help us do some of these things – to a certain extent.

DNA AND GENES

The human body is composed of several trillion cells, each of which has a nucleus consisting of 46 string-like structures called chromosomes. These were discovered in Austria in the middle of the 19th century by an Augustinian monk named Gregor Mendel.

The chromosomes come in two sets, one set inherited from each parent. Of the 23 chromosomes in each set, 22 of these will be single chromosomes, while the remainder will be one of the sex chromosomes X or Y. A woman's cells contain two X chromosomes, and a man's an X and a Y chromosome, the latter being inherited from his father (which is significant for family history).

Each chromosome contains tightly coiled threads of deoxyribonucleic acid (DNA) and associated protein molecules. The DNA, which was first identified by the Swiss biochemist Friederich Meischer in 1869 and named 'nuclein', contains (in the form of genes) the instructions to our bodies for our physical characteristics, which can then be passed on to future generations. After work by the British bacteriologist Fred Griffith in the 1920s, and later by the American scientist Theodore Avery, DNA was finally accepted by the scientific community in 1952 as the transmitter of inheritance.

A DNA molecule in humans and other higher organisms comprises two strands wrapping round each other like a twisted ladder (the double-helix), whose 'rungs' consisting of chemicals containing nitrogen are called bases. There are four bases in DNA: adenine (A), thymine (T), cytosine (C) and guanine (G). Genes are discrete stretches of these bases that code the instructions for the body, and in humans the genes take up only about 5-10 per cent of the DNA. The genes are, in effect, units of heredity information.

The double-helix format of DNA was discovered by James Watson and Francis Crick in Cambridge in 1953, based on experimental work carried out in London by Rosalind Franklin and Maurice Wilkins. Watson, Crick and Wilkins shared the Nobel Prize for Physiology or Medicine in 1962. Franklin had previously died of cancer in 1958 (at the age of 37).

The entire heritable genetic material in the chromosomes is known as the genome. There are around 24,000 genes in the human genome, with each gene having a fixed position on a chromosome. A project to 'sequence the human genome' was completed by 14 April 2003, ahead of its original 2005 target.

The aim of the Human Genome Project was to locate every human gene, determine its precise chemical structure, and find out its function in health and disease, in order to determine the genetic basis of human disease. The information gathered by the project will be the basic reference for research in human biology and medicine.

THE Y CHROMOSOME AND FAMILY HISTORY

Finding out about the genetic structure of humans may be of tremendous importance to medicine, but what's it got to do with family history? The answer is that, as humans inherit one half of their genetic information from their mothers and the other half from their fathers, their genetic structure ought to be useful to us in tracing our ancestry, and so it is.

At conception, the embryo receives one of the sex chromosomes from the mother (which will always be an X chromosome) and one from the father (which may be either X or Y). The Y chromosome contains a gene that causes a human embryo to become male, whereas it would otherwise be female.

The Y chromosome is inherited by a man from his father, who inherited it from his father, and so on back into the mists of time. Over the generations, the Y chromosome gradually changes. Definable segments (known as markers) can be detected in DNA tests, and compared to those of other men. When there is a close match in the results, it will indicate (depending on the number of markers tested) how long ago the two shared a common ancestor.

What it unfortunately won't do is tell you who that common ancestor was. Also, although the Y chromosome is usually passed from father to son unchanged, it does sometimes mutate. (If it didn't, all men would have exactly the same Y chromosome.) This means that two brothers may not match exactly, while two distant cousins may do so.

Even an exact match on 25 markers indicates only that there's a 50 per cent likelihood that the time to the most recent common ancestor (TMRCA) is seven generations or less, a 90 per cent likelihood that TMRCA is 23 generations ago or less, and a 95 per cent likelihood that TMRCA is 30 generations ago (i.e. 750-1,000 years ago, if we assume there are 3-4 generations in 100 years). These figures are based on the expectation that a marker will mutate once in 500 generations, which is the average of a number of studies.

Now, while it's interesting to know that you and someone else have a common ancestor who lived that number of years ago, it's not exactly very accurate. This information does give you an idea of how closely one man is related to another, however. Having found that out, you can then carry out detailed family history research of the traditional paper-based kind to find out who that common ancestor was.

MITOCHONDRIAL DNA

Women are no doubt thinking that this is all very well if you're a man, but what if you're female and have no Y chromosome to compare with others. You could always get a male relative to take a Y-chromosome DNA test, but it can't be your son, and how can you be absolutely sure that you and your brother share the same father? DNA testing can bring all sorts of skeletons out of the cupboard!

You can have your mitochondrial DNA (mtDNA) tested, however. This is DNA that isn't contained in the nucleus of a cell, but in the mitochondria, which are found in an area of the cell called the cytoplasm. Both men and women have mtDNA, but this is always inherited from your mother (although paternally-inherited mito-chondrial DNA *was* found in the muscle of a patient who had maternally-inherited mtDNA in his blood). In a similar way to Y-chromosome DNA, MtDNA mutates over the years, and can also be used to determine relationships.

DNA-TESTING WEB SITES

There are several websites that have been set up by companies that will carry out DNA testing for you. Among these are the UK-based **Oxford Ancestors** (www.oxfordancestors.com), founded by Brian Sykes, Professor of Human Genetics at Oxford University in England, which offers both an mtDNA test and a Y-chromosome test based on ten markers.

If you have the Y-chromosome test done, you can also have a test carried out to see whether your DNA matches what the company calls the 'Tribes of Britain' (i.e.

Home page of Oxford Ancestors.

the ancient peoples of Britain). According to Oxford Ancestors, in the male population of the British Isles today, three ancient peoples account for the origins of 95
per cent of Y-chromosome DNA: the Celts, the Anglo-Saxons/Danish Vikings and
the Norse Vikings. The DNA of the Anglo-Saxons and the Danes is too similar for
them to be classified separately.

Family Tree DNA (www.familytreedna.com), based in the United States, carries
out both mtDNA and Y-chromosome tests, where the basic tests are similar to those
provided by Oxford Ancestors (the Y-chromosome test is based on 12 markers). Family Tree DNA also provides Y-chromosome tests using 25 and 37 markers, as well
as an mtDNA test on a larger section of DNA. The greater the number of markers
covered in a test, the more recent will be the time to the most recent common
ancestor (TMRCA) of two people whose results match on all the markers.

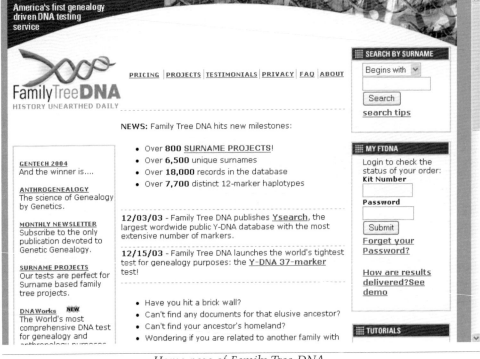

Home page of Family Tree DNA.

As well as mtDNA and 26-marker Y-chromosome tests, **GeneTree** (www.genetree.
com) carries out home (16-marker), legal, and pre-natal DNA paternity testing as
well. The company also provides full- or half-siblingship, grandparentage, first-cousin,
and aunt or uncle testing, as well as an analysis of whether twins are identical (from
one egg and one sperm) or fraternal (two eggs and two sperms).

Another US-based company that offers mtDNA and 26-marker Y-chromosome
tests is **Relative Genetics** (www.relativegenetics.com), which also provides the op-

tion for a group of people to participate in a 'Family Genetics' project. In addition, Family Tree DNA, GeneTree and Relative Genetics all offer Native American ancestry-validation services. Family Tree DNA's Y-chromosome test service also lets you check your results against known African and Cohanim (the hereditary Jewish priesthood of Biblical times) results.

Family Tree DNA hosts a discussion forum on its website, as does Oxford Ancestors, which also provides searchable databases of its mtDNA and Y-chromosome test results. Family Tree DNA provides a searchable database of Y-chromosome results. The companies' customers are then able to contact other customers with matching results, if they wish.

MOLECULAR GENEALOGY RESEARCH PROJECT

So far, the testing services that are publicly available have been confined to analysing the DNA in the Y chromosome and in the mitochondria. A more ambitious study – the Molecular Genealogy Research Project (MGRP) – is being carried out in the United States by the Sorenson Molecular Genealogy Foundation (SMGF) (www.smgf. org).

Through the MGRP, the foundation is building a database to let people enhance and extend their genealogical research through the use of genetics. The SMGF is not only looking at the Y-chromosome and mitochondrial DNA inheritance patterns, but also at the remaining chromosomes in the cell nucleus.

The project's mission is to collect genealogical DNA samples to create what it expects to be the world's most comprehensive correlated genetic and genealogical database. The foundation aims to provide funding to allow genetic tools for family history research to be constructed from the information in the database.

The MGRP's first task is collecting 100,000 DNA samples and genealogies from people over 18 who can provide a complete pedigree chart for a minimum of four generations. The SMGF expects to reach this initial goal by 2005.

SCOTTISH DNA PROJECTS

A number of Scottish DNA projects are in progress, such as the MacGregor DNA Project (www.clangregor.com/macgregor/dna.html). This has identified several branches of the clan as descending from Gregor, the name-father of the clan, who lived in the 14th century.

At the Official Clan Donnachaidh website (www.donnachaidh.com) you can read about the clan's DNA project, which it's hoped will establish whether the clan (whose main surname is Robertson) is descended from the Celtic Earls of Atholl or from Somerled, Lord of the Isles in the 12th century, who was the ancestor of the MacDonalds.

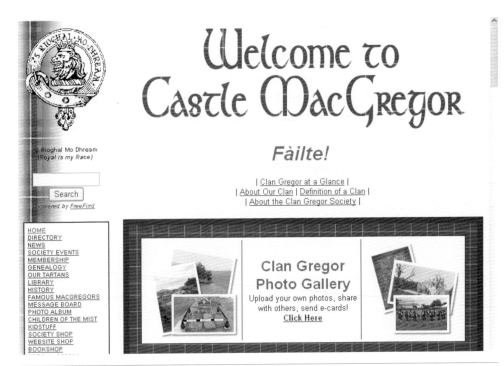

Home page of the Clan Gregor Society.

While carrying out research into genetic links between the Scots and the Norse Vikings for his book *Adam's Curse*, Professor Sykes found a number of participants in his Y-chromosome DNA testing programme had identical results. These were men with the surnames MacDonald, MacAlister and MacDougall, who Professor Sykes thought might all be descended from Somerled. This was proved when the DNA of the clan chiefs (who *did* descend from Somerled) was also tested, and found to match that of 20 per cent of their clansmen.

You can find the Stewart/Stuart DNA Project at www.angelfire.com/nb/stewartdna/. Most of the participants in the project live in the United States. As this project has a link on the Stewart Society's web page (www.stewartsociety.org), it would be useful if the society encouraged more Stewarts to participate. Then I might be able to find out if I am descended from the Appin Stewarts! (See section on the clans in Chapter 13.)

DNA AND TRADITIONAL FAMILY HISTORY

So does DNA testing mean the end of traditional family history? By no means. DNA testing can be a very helpful aid to family history research, but it won't give you the names of your most recent ancestors. For that you still need to search the written records. However, watch this space! In a few years time, we may see some very interesting results from the Molecular Genealogy Research Project.

Who knows? Maybe we *will* be able to check our DNA results against a table of those for Scottish kings and ancient clan chiefs. In a hundred years' time this may have become the standard way of finding who your ancestors were. Perhaps Robert the Bruce will turn out to have been every Scot's ancestor all along!

16 Online Records and Indexes for England and Wales

INTRODUCTION

The main chapters of this book describe the websites where you'll find records and indexes related to your Scottish ancestors. For the last 400 years, however, Scotland and England have shared the same monarch, and since 1707, the same parliament. Unsurprisingly, very many of the Scots who have left their homeland over the years have remained in Britain and gone 'down South' to England, and also to Wales (particularly to work in the South Wales coalfields).

According to the census of 2001, the population of England and Wales included over 800,000 Scots (and correspondingly, 8.4 per cent of the Scottish population had been born in England or Wales), so you may very well find that your ancestors crossed the Anglo-Scottish border.

Here then is a fairly brief description of some useful websites for ancestry research in England and Wales. You might wonder why there's no Anglo-Welsh equivalent of the *ScotlandsPeople* site with digitised images of birth, marriage and death records. Part of the reason lies in the relative size of the countries. In 1801 England and Wales taken together had five times the population of Scotland; two hundred years later, their combined size is ten times as great as that of their northern neighbour.

Also, Scotland now has its own devolved government, while England doesn't. The General Register Office for Scotland (GROS) has undertaken a major project to transform the way in which it makes records publicly available. This is known as DIGROS (the Digital Imaging of the Genealogical Records of Scotland's people). The GROS received £3 million-worth of funding from the Scottish Executive specifically to cover the three-year DIGROS programme.

1901 CENSUS FOR ENGLAND AND WALES

Although neither the civil registration births, marriages and deaths nor the baptisms, banns and burials from the parish registers have been digitised, two of the censuses for England and Wales have been: that for 1901 by The National Archives (formerly the Public Record Office) and its contractors, and the 1891 census through the online genealogy provider *Ancestry.co.uk.*

The 1901 census was supposed to have been available on the Web by January 2002, but the online implementation was beset by problems, principally because it wasn't robust enough to be accessed by around 30 million people on day one. The 1901 census website (www.census.pro.gov.uk) finally went live in September 2002, after many months of alterations and testing.

The Anglo-Welsh search differs from the Scottish in certain respects. First of all, you can search in the former free of charge: you pay only when you want to see a transcript of a census record or an image of the actual page from the handwritten enumeration. (See Appendix 1.)

In addition, the search function of the Anglo-Welsh 1901 census has certain facilities that are absent from the Scottish search. You can, for example, search for people in England and Wales based on a forename only, whereas a search in Scotland requires a surname to be entered. In addition, in the Anglo-Welsh census, you can search for someone according to where he or she was born. This facility is missing from the Scottish search.

ANCESTRY.CO.UK

After the bad publicity generated by the delay in putting the 1901 census for England and Wales online, The National Archives signed a licence agreement with *Ancestry. co.uk* (the UK arm of the American family history services provider *Ancestry.com*) for the censuses from 1841-1891 to go online as part of *Ancestry's* subscription service for the UK (see Appendix 1). The 1891 census is now available through *Ancestry* (www.ancestry.co.uk) for England, Wales, the Isle of Man and the Channel Islands, and the company began putting the 1871 census up at the beginning of 2004.

The search facility for the 1871 and 1891 censuses is similar to that described above for The National Archives' 1901 census, allowing searches on forename and place of birth. If you specify an age, however, it must be specific, whereas the 1901 search will accept an age +/- any number of years. Entering an exact age can be a problem, however. You may know exactly when the person you're looking for was born: he or she may not have known or, at least, not wanted to admit it. It's quite amazing how so many people aged by only six to eight years between censuses!

Another useful index for England and Wales that's been made available online through *Ancestry* is Pallot's Marriage Index. This covers 1.7 million marriages that took place between 1780 and 1837, mostly in London or Middlesex. It also includes marriages from 2,500 parishes in 38 other counties, however, including some in Wales.

FREECEN

The *FreeCEN* project (to provide online access free of charge to census records for 1841-1871 and 1891) was started in 1999 as part of the *FreeUKGEN* initiative, which also includes *FreeBMD* (see below) and *FreeREG* (which will provide a free index to entries in the parish registers of England and Wales).

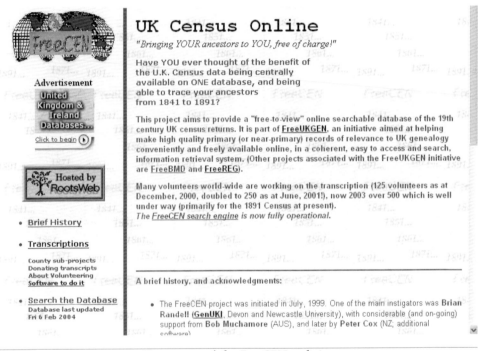

Home page of the FreeCEN website.

Although *FreeCEN* (freecen.rootsweb.com) covers Scotland as well as England and Wales, to a large extent the work of the project has been overtaken by events, as all the Scottish censuses from 1841-1871 are now being indexed and are expected to become available via the *ScotlandsPeople* website during 2004 (see Chapter 2). Still, accessing census returns on *FreeCEN* is free of charge (whereas you pay for access to the index and records at *ScotlandsPeople*), so *FreeCEN* is still worth bearing in mind for those Scottish census records that are available there. Note that there's no 'www' in the web address.

The same comments apply as far as the censuses from 1841-1891 for England, Wales, the Isle of Man and the Channel Islands are concerned, as the 1891 census has since been made available online by *Ancestry* (see above), and the 1841-1871 censuses are following. Until these are all online, however, *FreeCEN* will remain the only major source of census returns on the Web for England and Wales.

It's worth while, however, carrying out a general search for a location in England or Wales using a search-engine such as Google, as some individuals have posted census returns for particular areas on the Web. If you search for 'Lydney 1851 census', for instance, you'll find that it's been put up on RootsWeb by Gordon Beavington. If you simply search for '1871 census', among the results you'll find the returns for Matlock and Matlock Bath in Derbyshire, which have been put up online by Ann Andrews.

DOCUMENTSONLINE

The entire collection of over a million wills proved by the Prerogative Court of Canterbury (PCC) between 1384 and 1858 have been put up online by The National Archives at www.documentsonline.pro.gov.uk. The PCC's area of jurisdiction

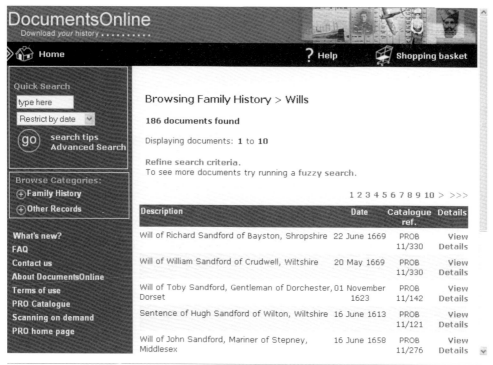

Results of a search for wills.

covered what was originally the ecclesiastical province of Canterbury, which was the southern half of England and most of Wales. In addition, wills made by English and Welsh people overseas were often proved at the PCC.

As with the Scottish wills at *ScottishDocuments* (see Chapter 4), the *DocumentsOnline* index can be searched free of charge, although there *is* a charge for downloading the image of a will (see Appendix 1). The search can be by surname, forename, place, occupation – there are 2,609 wills by labourers – or date, or any combination of these.

In early 2004, an index of five and a half million soldiers who were awarded campaign medals in the First World War was added to the *DocumentsOnline* website. The information, taken from index cards created by the Army Medal Office towards the end of the war, is being put online in alphabetical batches according to the soldiers' surnames. All of the cards, including those for women and people 'mentioned in despatches', were expected to be online by the end of 2004.

FAMILY RESEARCH LINK

Although the civil registration records of births, marriages and deaths for England and Wales haven't been digitised, it *is* at least possible to search the indexes for these records, and then to place an online order for the certificates. Title Research, a company that provides probate and succession genealogy services to lawyers as well as corporate and public trustees around the world, had computerised the Anglo-Welsh birth, marriage and death indexes for its own use.

The firm then decided to offer these on the Internet as a pay-as-you-go service through its sister company Family Research Link (see Appendix 1). An online version of the paper or microfiche indexes is accessible online at Family Research Link's website (www.1837online.com), covering the period 1837-1983. Births, marriages and deaths which took place after 1983 can be searched for in a fully computerised index. Deaths after 1983 can also be searched by subscribers to Ancestry.co.uk (see above).

FREEBMD

The online indexes provided by Family Research Link, which can be viewed online in your own home, are a huge improvement on having to go to a library or record office and trying to read poorly-produced microfiches in negative format. Nevertheless, these are still the same indexes that were originally available on paper, with no full database search facility.

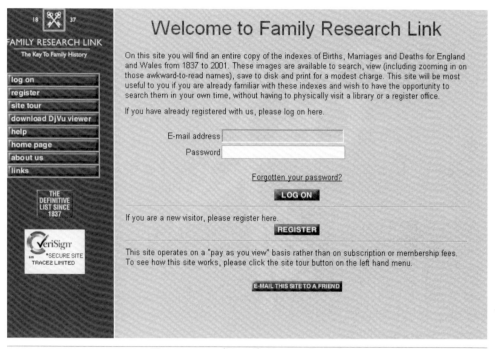

Home page of Family Research Link

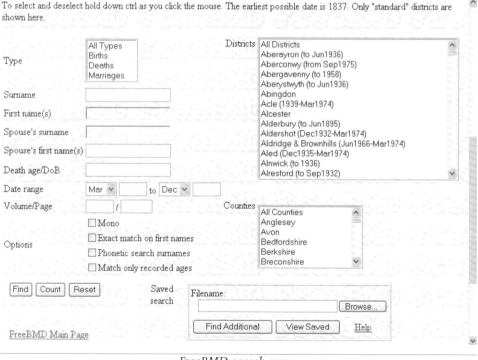

FreeBMD search page.

The *FreeBMD* project aims to create just such a fully-searchable database, and has been working towards this since 1998. The database is expected to be complete by 2007, but, in the meantime, around 2.5 million records are being added every month. The database can be searched at freebmd.rootsweb.com. Note there's no 'www' in the web address.

CERTIFICATE ORDERING SERVICE

Once you've found the reference number for the certificate you want, you can order it through the online ordering service of the General Register Office for England and Wales (GRO) at www.col.statistics.gov.uk. You can also pay for it online – at a lower charge than if you order by post or phone. (See Appendix 1.)

FAMILYHISTORYONLINE

The Federation of Family History Societies (FFHS) has put on to the Web on a pay-per-view basis (see Appendix 1) various databases compiled by local family history societies in England and Wales. At the *FamilyHistoryOnline* website (www. familyhistoryonline.net), you can search indexes of baptisms, marriages, burials,

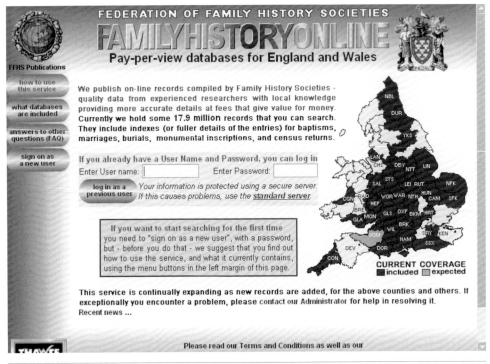

Home page of FamilyHistoryOnline.

monumental inscriptions and census returns. Most English counties are covered, as are several in Wales.

ENGLISH ORIGINS

English Origins is provided by Origins.net as a sister service to *Scots Origins* (see Chapter 9) and *Irish Origins*. At its website (www.englishorigins.com), you can search in a number of indexes provided by the Society of Genealogists (www.sog.org.uk). These include Boyd's Marriage Index, which contains over 6.4 million names from 1538 to 1840, and several other indexes of wills, London apprenticeship abstracts, and other records. The indexes are accessible on a pay-per-view basis, with special discounts for members of the Society of Genealogists. (See Appendix 1.)

17 Visiting Scotland and Searching in Local Archives

INTRODUCTION

Although this book is about tracing your Scottish ancestry from a distance using the Internet, I don't want to suggest that those of you who don't live in Scotland needn't bother going there at all. Yes, you can do more and more of the research from home, but I hope you become so fascinated with what your ancestors were doing that you'll want to go and see for yourself where they lived. Plus, you can visit local archives and museums to find out more about your ancestors and how people lived in the past in different parts of Scotland.

Although you can get a tremendous amount of information from the Web, and from books and magazines, you'll only get the 'feel' of Scotland if you visit it yourself and meet the people. And eat the food. And drink the drink. When you've experienced Scottish weather at its most miserable (I hope you don't), you'll understand why it feels so good to warm yourself up with a bowl of porridge or a 'wee dram' of malt whisky. Not that the weather's poor in Scotland all the time. By no means, and the countryside and cities look very beautiful in a rugged way, when the sun shines.

You certainly won't be alone when you visit Scotland. A report published in 2003 by the Ancestral Tourism Industry Steering Group revealed that in 2001 over a quarter of a million tourists went there to trace their family trees. 'Ancestral tourism' is very important for Scotland, as those tourists contribute £153 million to the country's economy. The authors of the report believe that the number of ancestral tourists could well triple in the coming years.

Even before family history became as popular as it is today, Scotland was keen to promote itself as the land of history, which it certainly is. Wherever you go, you're bound to come across something old and interesting. The Ancestral Scotland website (www.ancestralscotland.com) aims to encourage people with Scottish ancestry to visit Scotland, and contains many articles about the Scots and genealogy. There are also links to other articles on the Visit Scotland website www.visitscotland.com, the official site of Scotland's National Tourism Board.

LOCAL ARCHIVES

Although the main records you need to look at to trace your Scottish ancestry are held in Edinburgh at New Register House (the General Register Office for Scotland (GROS), and the Court of the Lord Lyon) and at General Register House (the National Archives of Scotland (NAS)), there's a lot of other useful information held in local archives.

The biggest of these are in Scotland's other major cities: Glasgow (population 629,501 at the 2001 census), Aberdeen (184,788) and Dundee (154,674), while Edinburgh (430,082) has other archives with records relating to the city and its environs. Inverness, while having a population of only 40,949, has long been considered the 'capital of the Highlands', and also holds an important archive.

ABERDEEN LOCAL ARCHIVES

Aberdeen City Archives (www.aberdeencity.gov.uk/acc_data/information/arc_main. asp) holds the city's family history resources in two locations: Town House and Old Aberdeen House. At the Archives website, you can download a pdf copy of a helpful leaflet entitled 'Family History Resources in the City Archives'.

The Reference and Local Studies Department of **Aberdeen City Library** (www. aberdeencity.gov.uk/acc_data/service/arts_refloc2.asp) also holds collections of newspapers, maps, photographs and various other items of interest to family historians.

DUNDEE LOCAL ARCHIVES

The Local Studies department of **Dundee Central Library** (www.dundeecity.gov.uk/ centlib/locindex.html) holds over 20,000 printed items relating to Dundee, as well as prints, photographs, postcards, maps and plans.

The **Dundee City Archive & Record Centre** (www.dundeecity.gov.uk/archives) holds official records, as well as church, family, estate, business, trade union and other private records.

The **Friends of Dundee City Archives** (www.fdca.org.uk) supports the work of the archivists through subscriptions and fund-raising activities. As well as running lunchtime talks, publishing a newsletter, and arranging social events and outings, the group has created online databases of:

- Wesleyan register of baptisms, Dundee 1785-1898 (www.fdca.org.uk/methodists. htm)

- Burial records for the Howff cemetery, Dundee (www.fdca.org.uk/howff.htm)

- Vehicle registration records for the counties of Perth (1909-1911) and Kinross (1904-1952) (www.fdca.org.uk/registrations.htm)

- Poor registers for Liff and Benvie (1854-1865) and Dundee East Poorhouse (www.fdca.org.uk/poor_index.htm)

A special Genealogy Unit has been set up by the **Dundee Registrar of Births, Deaths and Marriages** (www.dundeecity.gov.uk/registrars/genindex.htm) for people who want to trace their ancestry in the Dundee and Angus area. You can either go in person to carry out a search with the aid of a registrar, or make a postal or email application.

Dundee City Council's **Leisure & Arts Department** (www.dundeecity.gov.uk/leisureandarts/main.htm) holds records of 19th-century burials in the city's three main burial grounds: Balgay/Western Necropolis, Western Cemetery and Eastern Necropolis, all of which are still in use.

EDINBURGH LOCAL ARCHIVES

Edinburgh City Archives (www.edinburgh.gov.uk/CEC/Corporate_Services/Corporate_Communications/archivist/Edinburgh_City_Archives.html) in the City Chambers, headquarters of Edinburgh City Council, holds political, administrative, judicial, business, personal, domestic, criminal, religious, social, legal and commercial information relating to the city, and dating as far back as 1130.

The Edinburgh Room at **Edinburgh Central Library** (www.edinburgh.gov.uk/libraries/edinburghroom/edinburghroom.html) holds over 100,000 books, maps, prints, slides, parish registers, census records and newspaper cuttings about Edinburgh. As well as information on Edinburgh itself, the holdings also include information on parts of the city that were once separate entities.

The Edinburgh Room's collection of **illustrations** includes prints, photographs, original paintings, drawings, lantern slides and slides (which can be borrowed). These cover all periods, and include scenes, events, portraits and subjects. Around 2,000 of the collection's illustrations of Edinburgh Old Town can be viewed on the website of the Scottish Cultural Resources Access Network (SCRAN) at www.scran.ac.uk.

GLASGOW LOCAL ARCHIVES

The **Mitchell Library** in Glasgow is the home of both a **Family History Centre** (www.glasgowlibraries.org/familyhistoryarchives.htm) (within the Special Collections section of Archives and Special Collections) and **Glasgow City Archives** (www.glasgowlibraries.org/archives.htm). The City Archives hold the records of the former Glasgow Corporation, as well as most county and parish records for places within the pre-1996 Strathclyde Region.

The **Strathclyde Area Genealogy Centre** (www.glasgow.gov.uk/html/council/dept/protect/genealogy/) holds copies of records covering the area of the former Strathclyde Region. These are the Statutory Registers of Births, Deaths and Marriages

(1855-1992) on microfiche, as well as the census records from 1841 to 1891 and the pre-1855 Old Parish Registers on microfilm. In addition, the Genealogy Centre has a computer link to the GROS indexes in Edinburgh.

INVERNESS LOCAL ARCHIVES

The **Highland Council Archive** (www.highland.gov.uk/educ/publicservices/archive-details/highlandarchive.htm) in Inverness holds the official records of the present Highland Council, but also those of its pre-1996 predecessors: the Highland Regional Council and eight district councils, as well as those of the five pre-1975 counties: Caithness, Sutherland, Ross and Cromarty, Inverness and Nairn. The Highland Council Archive also includes a photographic archive, a major part of which is the Whyte Collection of around 140,000 items.

The **North Highland Archive** (www.highland.gov.uk/educ/publicservices/archive-details/northarchive.htm) in Wick is responsible for the records of the county of Caithness and the towns of Wick and Thurso. Both Archives operate Genealogical Centres.

In addition, the **Registrar of Births, Deaths and Marriages** (www.highland.gov.uk/landaintra/corporate_services/registrar/ancestry.htm) in Inverness runs Ancestry Research centres in the area registration offices in Inverness, Dingwall, Fort William, Thurso, Wick and Portree, the first four of which have a computer link to the GROS indexes in Edinburgh. The Inverness area office holds Statutory Registers of Births, Deaths and Marriages from 1855 to 1965 for the former county of Inverness.

JEWISH ARCHIVES

The **Scottish Jewish Archives Centre** (www.sjac.org.uk) holds a database with information on 23,000 Jews who lived in Scotland before the Second World War. The information comes from over 70 sources, including cemetery records, synagogue registers, naturalisations, charity subscription lists, and school admission registers.

Opened in 1987, the centre is a national heritage, information and research centre, which also contains an exhibition of the history of Jews in Scotland since the 17th century. The centre holds records of the larger Jewish communities in Edinburgh (founded in 1816), Glasgow (1823), Aberdeen and Dundee, as well as those of the small communities which used to exist in Ayr, Dunfermline, Falkirk, Greenock and Inverness.

OTHER ARCHIVES IN SCOTLAND

The website of the Scottish Archive Network (SCAN) (www.scan.org.uk) contains a directory of Scottish archives, covering those of local authorities, businesses, clans, health boards, universities, art schools and various other organisations (such as the

SCAN online catalogue page.

National Monuments Record of Scotland, National Trust for Scotland, Royal College of Nursing, Royal College of Physicians and Surgeons of Glasgow, Royal College of Surgeons of Edinburgh, and Scottish Catholic Archive.) The catalogues of 52 of Scotland's archives can be searched using an online facility at SCAN's website.

You can find out what other libraries in Scotland hold (and also those in the rest of the UK and the Irish Republic) at the Familia website (www.familia.org.uk). Familia describes itself as a web-based directory of family history resources held in public libraries in the UK and Ireland.

There's certainly a large number of archives and libraries for you to search in when you visit Scotland. Let's hope, though, that over the coming years more of their records, or at least their indexes, will become accessible over the Internet. Happy hunting for your ancestors!

Appendix 1
Charges for Access to Online Indexes and Records

1901 Census (for England and Wales)
£5 for a 48-hour session. As part of the £5 charge, it costs 50p to view a transcription of an individual person's entry, 50p more to view a transcription of the rest of the people in the same household, or 75p to view the digital image of a page from the census returns.

Achievements of Canterbury (Gretna Green Marriage Index)
£15 for full details of a marriage. Extractions of further entries are at a rate of £40 per 12 entries pro rata.

Ancestry.co.uk
Subscription to the UK and Ireland Collection:

- Annually: £69.95, US$99.95, Can$159.95, or Aus$199.95;
- Quarterly: £29.95, US$39.95, Can$59.95, or Aus$79.95.

Court of the Lord Lyon
Cost of applying for a coat of arms:

- New Grant of Armorial Bearings, including shield alone, with or without motto – £850;
- New Grant of Armorial Bearings, including shield and crest, with or without motto – £1,303;
- New Grant of Armorial Bearings, including shield, crest, motto and supporters – £1,836;
- Matriculation of previously recorded Armorial Bearings, including shield and crest – £431;
- Matriculation of previously recorded Armorial Bearings, including shield and crest and supporters – £690;
- Matriculation of previously recorded Armorial Bearings, including shield and crest, together with Grant of new supporters – £953.

Documents Online
£3.50 to view a will or a medal card.

Dundee Genealogy Unit
£30 for a 2-hour visit, or £30 for compilation of a family tree by a member of staff, for which you can apply by post, email, or using the unit's online genealogy request form.

English Origins

- £6 for 300 credits, expiring after 7 days;
- £10 for 600 credits, expiring after 14 days.

One credit equals one index record. You can also pay £10 to order a hard copy of a source document.

FamilyHistoryOnline
Payments of £5, £10, £20 or £50 can be made online. As part of one of these charges, you can view entries in the databases at charges varying from 2p to 9p per record.

Family Research Link

- £5 for 50 units, which expire after 45 days;
- £25 for 300 units, which expire after 120 days;
- £60 for 800 units, which expire after 365 days;
- £120 for 2,400 units, which also expire after 365 days.

One unit equals one image page. If you purchase a new price plan before the old one expires, the outstanding units are then carried forward to the new expiry date.

General Register Office (for England & Wales) Certificate Ordering Service
£7 for order via website of full certificate of birth, marriage or death. £23 for priority service. (If you supply the full GRO index reference, it costs £8.50 for a full certificate by post, phone or fax, and £24.50 for the priority service.)

General Register Office for Scotland (GROS) Certificate Ordering Service
£8 for a certificate by post, telephone or fax (plus £5 more for a 'particular search', and £10 extra for priority delivery).

Highland Council Ancestry Research Centre (Registrar of Births, Deaths and Marriages)
General search for £10 (up to 1 hour, with an extra £5 for an additional hour). £5 for a 'particular search' for a specified entry over a five-year period. £12 per half-hour session of computer access to GROS indexes in Edinburgh.

Highland Council Genealogy Centre (Highland Council Archive)
£12 per hour for a genealogical consultation, up to a maximum of 3 hours. Postal enquiries are charged at:

- £20 for up to 1 hour's work;
- £35 for up to 2 hours' work;
- £50 for up to 3 hours' work.

The [UK] National Archives (Public Record Office)
£10 for an estimate for copying documents from up to five full references from the TNA/PRO catalogue.

Police and 'Black Sheep' Indexes
£6 for major police reports or 'black sheep' reports. £3 for minor police reports. Discounts on major reports: 2 for £10, 3 for £15, 4 for £20, 5 for £25, 6 for £30, and 7 for £35.

ScotlandsPeople
£6 for 30 'page credits' for a 48-hour period. When the session expires, credits are not lost, but added to those in the next 48-hour session purchased. £10 for an official printed copy of a record.

Scots Origins **Sighting Service**
£8 for the transcription of a statutory record, £9 for an Old Parish Register entry, and £12.50 for a census entry.

Scottish Documents
£5 to view a will or inventory, regardless of length.

Statistical Account of Scotland
£40 per year for the subscription service for non-academic users.

CHARGES FOR GENETIC TESTS

Family Tree DNA

- Y-chromosome (12 markers)   US$159
- Y-chromosome (25 markers)   US$229
- Y-chromosome (37 markers)   US$289
- mtDNA   US$219
- mtDNA (high resolution)   US$299

GeneTree

- Y-chromosome (26 markers)   US$225
- mtDNA   US$245

Oxford Ancestors

- Y-chromosome (10 markers)   £180
- mtDNA   £180

Relative Genetics

- Y-chromosome (26 markers)   US$225
- mtDNA   US$245

Most of these companies offer discounted prices for combinations of tests, and for group testing.

Appendix 2
Finding Scottish Parishes

PARISH REGISTERS

You can find information about the Scottish parishes on the website of the General Register Office for Scotland (GROS) (www.gro-scotland.gov.uk). If you click on 'Searching Historical Records' in the Family Records section, a page will be displayed with links to various interesting information, including a 'List of Old Parochial Records' (OPRs).

Click on this link, and you'll see a page headed 'List of the Old Parochial Registers'. If you then click on one of the 19 links (showing the parish numbers) for the historic counties or groups of them, you'll be taken to an online version of a printed document entitled 'Detailed List of the Old Parochial Registers of Scotland', which was first published in 1872.

If you don't know what county a parish was (mainly) in, you can click on the 'Index' link to find the parish's number. Although they're numbered from 1-901, there were actually more than that number of parishes in Scotland. You'll see that in the six pages of the index, some of the parish numbers have a suffix. Aberdeen, for example, is number 168a, and the neighbouring parish of Old Machar is 168b. Although Edinburgh's parish number is simply 685, its neighbours St Cuthberts and Canongate are numbers 685/2 and 685/3 respectively.

The 19 lists of parishes show between which years (up to 1854) there are baptism, marriage, and death records for each parish, indicated by the letters 'B', 'M', and 'D'. So, for example, you might be aware that the parish of Glenholm in Peeblesshire has parish records that begin in 1747, and indeed there are baptisms from 1747 right up to 1854, but marriages only for the years 1784-95, and deaths from 1783 to 1851. Not only are there obvious missing years, but the GROS warns that even covering years should be treated with caution, as their accuracy isn't guaranteed and they don't reflect gaps of months or years within them.

There are three appendices to the 19 detailed lists, which deal with:

1. Church of Scotland records in the National Archives of Scotland (NAS) that contain pre-1855 baptism, marriage and death entries. Some of these records supplement, wholly or partly, those in the GROS's OPRs.
2. Kirk session and other information found in the OPRs.
3. Miscellaneous records containing entries from non-conformist churches relevant to the OPRs.

COMMISSARY AND SHERIFF COURT AREAS

Having found which county a parish belongs to, you can then find lists showing which counties came under which commissary courts and which sheriff courts on the *Scottish Documents* website (www.scottishdocuments.com). Click on 'Research Tools', and then on

'Places in Scotland' on the page that displays. You'll then see on the 'Places in Scotland' page the following links:

- Counties and Sheriff Courts List;

- Counties and Commissariots;

- Commissariots and Counties.

You can also obtain information on the dates covered by the indexes to the commissary and sheriff courts in the National Archives of Scotland (NAS) fact sheet on 'Wills and Testaments'. This can be downloaded from the NAS website at www.nas.gov.uk/miniframe/fact_sheet/wills.pdf.

For more information about specific parishes, the *Scottish Documents* website also points you in the direction of *GENUKI* (see Chapter 9) and the Statistical Accounts of Scotland (see Chapter 10).

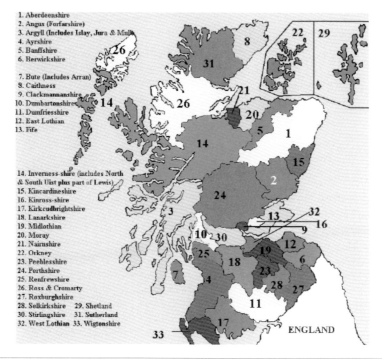

1. Aberdeenshire
2. Angus (Forfarshire)
3. Argyll (Includes Islay, Jura & Mull)
4. Ayrshire
5. Banffshire
6. Berwickshire

7. Bute (Includes Arran)
8. Caithness
9. Clackmannanshire
10. Dumbartonshire
11. Dumfriesshire
12. East Lothian
13. Fife

14. Inverness-shire (includes North & South Uist plus part of Lewis)
15. Kincardineshire
16. Kinross-shire
17. Kirkcudbrightshire
18. Lanarkshire
19. Midlothian
20. Moray
21. Nairnshire
22. Orkney
23. Peeblesshire
24. Perthshire
25. Renfrewshire
26. Ross & Cromarty
27. Roxburghshire
28. Selkirkshire   29. Shetland
30. Stirlingshire   31. Sutherland
32. West Lothian 33. Wigtonshire

Map of the historic counties of Scotland before 1975. (Map by Stephen Hew Browning.)

Appendix 3
Useful Addresses

Aberdeen City Archives

Town House   Old Aberdeen House
Broad Street   Dunbar Street
Aberdeen   AB10 1AQ   Aberdeen   AB24 3UJ
Telephone: +44 (0)1224 522513   Telephone: +44 (0)1224 481775
Website: www.aberdeencity.gov.uk/acc_data/information/arc_main.asp
Email: archives@aberdeencity.gov.uk   (See Chapter 17)

Aberdeen City Library

Reference & Local Studies
Central Library
Rosemount Viaduct
Aberdeen   AB25 1GW
Telephone: +44 (0)1224 652511/12/13
Website: www.aberdeencity.gov.uk/acc_data/service/arts_refloc2.asp
Email: refloc@arts-recaberdeen.net.uk   (See Chapter 17)

Association of Scottish Genealogists and Record Agents

51/3 Mortonhall Road
Edinburgh   EH9 2HN
Website: www.asgra.co.uk
(The ASGRA website contains a list of professional genealogists, who will carry out Scottish family history research for you, and their contact details.)

Court of the Lord Lyon

HM New Register House
3 West Register Street
Edinburgh   EH1 3YT
Website: www.lyon-court.com   (See Chapter 12)

Dundee Central Library

Local Studies Department
Wellgate Centre
Dundee   DD1 1DB
Telephone: +44 (0)1382 434377
Website: www.dundeecity.gov.uk/centlib/loc_stud.htm
Email: local.studies@dundeecity.gov.uk   (See Chapter 17)

Dundee City Archives
Archive & Record Centre
Support Services
21 City Square
Dundee   DD1 3BY
(Visitors enter by 1 Shore Terrace.)
Telephone: +44 (0)1382 434494
Website: www.dundeecity.gov.uk/archives/
Email: archives@dundeecity.gov.uk   (See Chapter 17)

Dundee Genealogy Unit
Registrar of Births, Deaths and Marriages
89 Commercial Street
Dundee   DD1 2AF
Telephone: +44 (0)1382 435222
Website: www.dundeecity.gov.uk/registrars/genealogy.html
Email: registrars@dundeecity.gov.uk   (See Chapter 17)

Dundee Leisure & Arts Department
Floor 13, Tayside House
28 Crichton Street
Dundee   DD1 3RA
Telephone: +44 (0)1382 433089
Website: www.dundeecity.gov.uk/leisureandarts/main.htm
Email: burials@dundeecity.gov.uk   (See Chapter 17)

Edinburgh City Archives
Department of Corporate Services
City of Edinburgh Council
City Chambers
High Street
Edinburgh   EH1 1YJ
Telephone: +44 (0)131 529 4616
Website: www.edinburgh.gov.uk/CEC/Corporate_Services/Corporate_Communications/
archivist/Edinburgh_City_Archives.html   (See Chapter 17)

Edinburgh City Libraries
Edinburgh Room
George IV Bridge
Edinburgh   EH1 1EG
Telephone: +44 (0)131 242 8030
Website: www.edinburgh.gov.uk/libraries/edinburghroom/edinburghroom.html
Email: edinburgh.room@edinburgh.gov.uk   (See Chapter 17)

General Register Office for Scotland (GROS)
HM New Register House
3 West Register Street
Edinburgh   EH1 3YT
Switchboard: +44 (0)131 334 0380
Certificate Ordering Service: +44 (0)131 314 4411
Website: www.gro-scotland.gov.uk
Email: records@gro-scotland.gov.uk   (See Chapters 1-3)

Glasgow City Archives
Mitchell Library
North Street
Glasgow   G3 7DN
Telephone: +44 (0)141 287 2913
Website: www.glasgowlibraries.org/archives.htm
Email: archives@cls.glasgow.gov.uk   (See Chapter 17)

Highland Council Archive
Cultural and Leisure Services
Inverness Library
Farraline Park
Inverness   IV1 1NH
Telephone: +44 (0)1463 220330
Website: www.highland.gov.uk/educ/publicservices/archivedetails/highlandarchive.htm
Email: archives@highland.gov.uk   (See Chapter 17)

Highland Council Ancestry Research Centre
Registrar of Births, Deaths and Marriages
Registration Office
Farraline Park
Inverness   IV1 1NH
Telephone: +44 (0)1463 239792
Website: www.highland.gov.uk/landaintra/corporate_services/registrar/ancestry.htm
Email: margaret.straube@highland.gov.uk   (See Chapter 17)

Mitchell Library
Family History Centre
North Street
Glasgow   G3 7DN
Telephone: +44 (0)141 287 2937
Website: www.glasgowlibraries.org/familyhistoryarchives.htm
Email: history_and_glasgow@cls.glasgow.gov.uk   (See Chapter 17)

National Archives of Scotland (NAS) (formerly the Scottish Record Office)
Historical Search Room
H M General Register House
2 Princes Street
Edinburgh   EH1 3YY
Telephone: +44 (0)131 535 1334
Website: www.nas.gov.uk
Email: enquiries@nas.gov.uk   (See Chapters 4 and 11)

[UK] National Archives
Public Record Office
Kew
Richmond
Surrey   TW9 4DU
Telephone: +44 (0)20 8876 3444
Website: www.pro.gov.uk
Email: enquiry@nationalarchives.gov.uk   (See Chapter 6)

National Library of Scotland
George IV Bridge
Edinburgh   EH1 1EW
Switchboard: +44 (0)131 226 4531
Website: www.nls.uk; website (maps): www.nls.uk/maps/index.html
Email: enquiries@nls.uk
(The holdings of the National Library of Scotland include a wonderful collection of Scottish maps, many of which are accessible on the Internet. The maps span the period 1560-1928, including Timothy Pont's maps made in the 1580s and 1590s, some 18th-century military maps, and Ordnance Survey maps from 1847 to 1895.)

North Highland Archive
Wick Library
Sinclair Terrace
Wick
Caithness   KW1 5AB
Telephone: +44 (0)1955 606432
Website: www.highland.gov.uk/educ/publicservices/archivedetails/northarchive.htm
E-mail: brenda.lees@highland.gov.uk   (See Chapter 17)

Registers of Scotland
Edinburgh Customer Service Centre   Glasgow Customer Service Centre
Erskine House   9 George Square
68 Queen Street   Glasgow   G2 1DY
Edinburgh   EH2 4NF
Telephone (Edinburgh): +44 (0)845 607 0161
Telephone (Glasgow): +44 (0)845 607 0164 or +44 (0)141 306 4425
Website: www.ros.gov.uk
Email: customer.services@ros.gov.uk   (See Chapter 11)

Scottish Jewish Archives Centre
Garnethill Synagogue
129 Hill Street
Glasgow   G3 6UB
Telephone: +44 (0)141 332 4911
Website: www.sjac.org.uk
Email: archives@sjac.fsbusiness.co.uk   (See Chapter 17)

Strathclyde Area Genealogy Centre
22 Park Circus
Glasgow   G3 6BE
Telephone: +44 (0)141 287 8364
Website: www.glasgow.gov.uk/html/council/dept/protect/genealogy/   (See Chapter 17)

Appendix 4
Useful Websites

A. WEBSITES MENTIONED BY CHAPTER

Part One – Records Available Online

1. **Statutory Records (Civil Registration)**
   General Register Office for Scotland (GROS) www.gro-scotland.gov.uk
   ScotlandsPeople www.scotlandspeople.gov.uk
   Scotland On Line www.scotlandonline.com
2. **Census Records**
   ScotlandsPeople www.scotlandspeople.gov.uk
3. **Old Parish Registers**
   ScotlandsPeople www.scotlandspeople.gov.uk
4. **Wills and Inventories**
   Scottish Documents www.scottishdocuments.com
   Scottish Archive Network (SCAN) www.scan.org.uk

Part Two – Other Information and Indexes Available Online

5. **Emigration and Immigration Databases**
   Highlands and Islands Emigration Society database www.scan.org.uk/researchtools/
      emigration.htm
   Ellis Island Immigration Museum www.ellisisland.com
   American Family Immigration History Center (Ellis Island database) www.ellisland.org
   Pier 21 information site www.pier21.ca
   National Archives of Canada databases www.archives.ca
   Cyndi's List of Genealogy Sites on the Internet www.cyndislist.com
   State Records Authority of New South Wales www.records.nsw.gov.au
   Archives Office of Tasmania www.archives.tas.gov.au/genealres/default.htm
   Public Record Office Victoria www.prov.vic.gov.au/access.htm
6. **UK National Archives Soldiers' Discharge Papers Index**
   PROCAT index catalogue.pro.gov.uk
   The [UK] National Archives (Public Record Office) www.pro.gov.uk
7. **East India Company Indexes**
   The Indiaman Magazine www.indiaman.com
   Cathy Day's *Family History in India* site members.ozemail.com.au/~clday/index.html
   Bob Holland's *Genealogy in India* site www.ans.com.au/~rampais/genelogy/india/index.
      htm

8. **Miscellaneous Indexes**

Scottish Strays Marriage Index www.m&lfhs.org.uk

Adobe Systems (for 'Acrobat' software) www.adobe.com

Commonwealth War Graves Commission Index www.cwgc.org

Gretna Green Index www.achievements.co.uk/services/gretna/index.php

Scottish Irregular and Runaway Marriages (list of custodians and owners of the records)
www.gro-scotland.gov.uk/grosweb/grosweb.nsf/pages/runmar

GROS paper on 'Marriages at Gretna, 1975-2000' www.gro-scotland.gov.uk/grosweb/grosweb.nsf/pages/occpgg

Derek Wilcox's police and 'black sheep' indexes www.lightage.demon.co.uk

9. **More Family History Websites, Mailing Lists and Discussion Groups**

LDS *FamilySearch* site www.familysearch.org

GENUKI site www.genuki.org.uk

Scots Origins www.scotsorigins.com

Hugh Wallis's IGI batch number search site freepages.genealogy.rootsweb.com/~hughwallis/IGIBatchNumbers.htm

RootsWeb www.rootsweb.com

Google Groups www.google.com/grphp

ScotlandsPeople Discussion Group www.scotlandspeople.gov.uk/phpBB/index.php

Yahoo! Groups uk.groups.yahoo.com

10. **The Statistical Accounts of Scotland**

Statistical Accounts of Scotland edina.ac.uk/statacc

Part Three – General Information

11. **Records at the National Archives of Scotland**

Scottish Archive Network (SCAN) online catalogue www.scan.org.uk/scan2003/aboutus/indexonline.htm

Registers of Scotland search request form www.ros.gov.uk/citizen/searchform.htm

National Archives of Scotland (NAS) factsheets www.nas.gov.uk/family_history.htm

National Archives of Scotland (NAS) online catalogue 195.153.34.3.dservea/

12. **Scottish Heraldry and the Records of the Lyon Court**

Court of the Lord Lyon www.lyon-court.com

Heraldry Society of Scotland www.heraldry-scotland.co.uk

List of 'Chiefs of Clans and Names' www.electricscotland.com/webclans/chiefs.htm

13. **The Scottish People: History, Clans and Names**

Scottish Parliament www.scottish.parliament.uk

GROS paper on 'Surnames in Scotland over the last 140 years' www.gro-scotland.gov.uk/grosweb/grosweb.nsf/pages/01surnames

GROS paper on 'Popular Forenames in Scotland, 1900-2000' www.gro-scotland.gov.uk/grosweb/grosweb.nsf/pages/name00

GROS paper on 'Popular Forenames in Scotland 2002' www.gro-scotland.gov.uk/grosweb/grosweb.nsf/pages/03names

14. **Scottish Family History Societies**

(See Appendix 5.)

15. **The Future of Family History: DNA**

Oxford Ancestors www.oxfordancestors.com

Family Tree DNA www.familytreedna.com
GeneTree www.genetree.com
Relative Genetics www.relativegenetics.com
Sorenson Molecular Genealogy Foundation www.smgf.org
MacGregor DNA Project www.clangregor.com/macgregor/dna.html
Official Clan Donnachaidh website www.donnachaidh.com
Stewart/Stuart DNA Project www.angelfire.com/nb/stewartdna/
Stewart Society www.stewartsociety.org

16. **Online Records and Indexes for England and Wales**
    1901 Census www.census.pro.gov.uk
    Ancestry.co.uk www.ancestry.co.uk
    FreeCEN (Free Census Project) freecen.rootsweb.com
    Documents Online www.documentsonline.pro.gov.uk
    Family Research Link www.1837online.com
    FreeBMD (Free Births, Marriages and Deaths Project) freebmd.rootsweb.com
    GRO (for England and Wales) Certificate Ordering Service www.col.statistics.gov.uk
    FamilyHistoryOnline www.familyhistoryonline.net
    English Origins www.englishorigins.com

17. **Visiting Scotland and Searching in Local Archives**
    Ancestral Scotland www.ancestralscotland.com
    Visit Scotland www.visitscotland.com
    (For web addresses of local archives, see Appendix 3.)

B. OTHER WEB SITES

Access to Archives (A2A) www.a2a.pro.gov.uk
('The English strand of the UK archives network.')

BBCi Scottish Roots www.bbc.co.uk/scotland/history/scottishroots/
(An online guide to 'Searching for your family history in Scotland'.)

British Library Net Family History Resources www.britishlibrary.net/family.html
(Links to family history websites, mainly in the UK.)

Burke's Peerage and Gentry www.burkes-peerage.net/sites/scotland/sitepages/clindex.asp
(The Scottish section of 'the definitive historical guide to the UK and Ireland's titled and landed families.' Contains interesting articles and a search facility.)

Burke's Peerage and Gentry Scottish Resources www.burkes-peerage.net/sites/common/sitepages/lisco.asp
(Links to Scottish genealogy and tourist websites.)

Census Online www.census-online.com
(Links to online census records, with over 38,000 in the United States.)

Electric Scotland www.electricscotland.com
('A major Scottish history site', which includes Family Tree, 'the world's largest genealogy publication, and the largest Scottish publication outside Scotland.')

FamilyRecords.gov.uk www.familyrecords.gov.uk
('Aims to help you find the UK government records and other sources you need for your family history research.')

Federation of Family History Societies www.ffhs.org.uk
(The 'umbrella' association for English and Welsh family history societies.)

Finding Family Roots on the Web www.msnbc.com/news/254376.asp
(Links to family history websites.)

Gazette Gateway www.gazettes-online.co.uk/
(Links to the London, Edinburgh and Belfast Gazettes, 'the official newspapers of record in the UK'.)

GenesConnected www.genesconnected.co.uk
(A sister site to Friends Reunited, the UK-based school and workplace reunion site.)

Roots Hebrides www.rootshebrides.com
('The first Web site dedicated to ancestry in the Outer Hebrides of Scotland.')

Rossbret Workhouse Site www.workhouses.co.uk
(Information about the former workhouses in England, Wales, Scotland and Ireland.)

ScotlandOnline.com Heritage www.scotlandonline.com/heritage
('The most comprehensive online collection of Scottish heritage information.')

The Workhouse users.ox.ac.uk/~peter/workhouse/index.html
(All about the former workhouses in England, Wales, Scotland and Ireland, with photographs of them as they are today.)

Appendix 5
Addresses and Websites of Members of SAFHS

A. SCOTTISH ASSOCIATION OF FAMILY HISTORY SOCIETIES (SAFHS)

(no postal address)
www.safhs.org.uk

B. FULL MEMBERS

Scotland

Aberdeen & North-East Scotland FHS
(covers the historic counties of Aberdeen, Banff, Kincardine and Moray (Elgin))
Family History Shop, 164 King Street, Aberdeen AB24 5BD
www.anesfhs.org.uk

Alloway & Southern Ayrshire FHS
c/o Alloway Public Library, Doonholm Road, Alloway, Ayr KA7 4QQ
www.asafhs.co.uk

Association of Scottish Genealogists & Record Agents
(association of professional searchers working personally in Scotland; the website contains a list of names and contact details)
51/3 Mortonhall Road, Edinburgh EH9 2HN
www.asgra.co.uk

Borders FHS
(covers the historic counties of Berwick, Peebles, Roxburgh and Selkirk)
The Toll House, Maxton, Melrose, Scottish Borders TD6 0RL
www.bordersfhs.org.uk

Caithness FHS
51 Upper Burnside Drive, Thurso, Caithness KW14 7XB
www.caithnessfhs.org.uk

Central Scotland FHS
(covers the former Central Region, i.e. the historic counties of Clackmannan and Stirling, the western part of Perthshire, and the former West Lothian parishes of Bo'ness and Carriden)
11 Springbank Gardens, Dunblane FK15 9JX
www.csfhs.org.uk

Dumfries & Galloway FHS
(covers the historic counties of Dumfries, Kirkcudbright and Wigtown)
9 Glasgow Street, Dumfries DG2 9AF
www.dgfhs.org.uk

East Ayrshire FHS
(covers the unitary authority of East Ayrshire, i.e. the former districts of Kilmarnock & Loudoun and Cumnock & Doon Valley)
c/o Dick Institute, Elmbank Avenue, Kilmarnock KA1 3BU
www.eastayrshire.org.uk

Fife FHS
Glenmoriston, Durie Street, Leven, Fife KY8 4HF
www.fifefhs.org

Glasgow & West of Scotland FHS
(covers the historic counties of Argyll, Ayr, Bute, Dunbarton, Lanark and Renfrew, and part of Stirlingshire)
Unit 5, 22 Mansfield Street, Glasgow G11 5QP
www.gwsfhs.org.uk

Heraldry Society of Scotland
(association promoting the study of heraldry and its correct use in Scotland)
25 Craigentinny Crescent, Edinburgh EH7 6QA
www.heraldry-scotland.co.uk

Highland Family History Society/Comunn Sloinntearachd Na Gaidhealtachd
(covers the Highland and Western Isles unitary authorities, i.e. the historic counties of Inverness, Nairn, Ross & Cromarty, and Sutherland)
c/o Reference Room, Public Library, Farraline Park, Inverness, IV1 1NH
www.genuki.org.uk/big/scot/Highland.FHS.home.html

Lanarkshire FHS
c/o Local History Room, Motherwell Heritage Centre, High Road, Motherwell, North Lanarkshire ML1 3HU
www.lanarkshirefhs.org.uk

Largs & North Ayrshire FHS
c/o Largs Library, 18 Allanpark Street, Largs, Ayrshire KA30 9AG
www.largsnafhs.org.uk

Lothians FHS
(covers the historic counties of West Lothian (Linlithgow), Midlothian (Edinburgh), and East Lothian (Haddington))
c/o Lasswade High School Centre, Eskdale Drive, Bonnyrigg, Midlothian EH19 2LA
www.lothiansfhs.org.uk

Orkney FHS
c/o Orkney Library & Archive, 44 Junction Rd, Kirkwall, Orkney KW15 1AG
www.orkneyfhs.org.uk

Renfrewshire FHS
c/o Paisley Museum & Art Galleries, High Street, Paisley PA1 2BA
www.renfrewshirefhs.org.uk

Scottish Genealogy Society
(association for family history research in Scotland as a whole)
15 Victoria Terrace, Edinburgh EH1 2JL
www.scotsgenealogy.com

Shetland FHS
6 Hillhead, Lerwick, Shetland ZE1 0ES
www.shetland-fhs.org.uk

Tay Valley FHS
(covers the historic counties of Angus, Fife, Kinross and Perth)
The Research Centre, 179-181 Princes Street, Dundee DD4 6DQ
www.tayvalleyfhs.org.uk

Troon @ Ayrshire FHS
c/o MERC, Troon Public Library, South Beach, Troon, Ayrshire KA10 6AF
www.troonayrshirefhs.org.uk

West Lothian FHS
23 Templar Rise, Livingston, West Lothian EH54 6PJ
www.wlfhs.org.uk

England

Anglo-Scottish FHS
(a sub-division of Manchester & Lancashire FHS)
Clayton House, 59 Piccadilly, Manchester MR1 2AQ
www.mlfhs.org.uk

Genealogical Society of Utah
(part of the Church of Jesus Christ of Latter-day Saints)
Family History Support Office, 185 Penns Lane, Sutton Coldfield B76 1JU
www.familysearch.org

Guild of One-Name Studies
(association of people researching all occurrences of particular surnames)
Box G, 14 Charterhouse Buildings, Goswell Road, London EC1M 7BA
www.one-name.org

Society of Genealogists
(association for family history research in the UK as a whole)
14 Charterhouse Buildings, Goswell Road, London EC1M 7BA
www.sog.org.uk

C. ASSOCIATE MEMBERS

Australia

Australian Institute of Genealogical Studies
(association for family history research in Australia as a whole)
PO Box 339, Blackburn, Victoria 3130
www.aigs.org.au

Queensland FHS
PO Box 171, Indooroopilly, Queensland 4068
www.qfhs.org.au

Scottish Ancestry Group, Genealogical Society of Victoria
Level 6, 179 Queen Street, Melbourne, Victoria 3000
www.gsv.org.au/sag.htm

Scottish Group, Genealogical Society of Queensland
PO Box 8423, Woolloongabba, Queensland 4102
www.gsq.org.au/society/scottish.html

Scottish Historical & Genealogical Research Group of Ballarat
Ballarat & District Genealogical Society
P.O. Box 1809, Ballarat Mail Centre, Victoria 3354
www.ballaratgenealogy.org.au

Scottish Interest Group, Western Australian Genealogical Society
6/48 May Street, Bayswater, Western Australia 6053
www.wags.org.au/groups/sigscot.htm

Shoalhaven FHS
PO Box 591, Nowra, New South Wales 2541
(no web address)

Society of Australian Genealogists
(association for family history research in Australia as a whole; has a Scottish Interest Group)
Richmond Villa, 120 Kent Street, Sydney, New South Wales 2000
www.sag.org.au

South Australian Genealogy & Heraldry Society
(has a Scottish Interest Group)
GPO Box 592, Adelaide, South Australia 5001
www.saghs.org.au

Heraldry & Genealogy Society of Canberra
(has a Scottish Interest Group)
GPO Box 585, Canberra, Australian Capital Territory 2601
www.hagsoc.org.au

Canada

British Columbia Genealogical Society
PO Box 88054, Lansdowne Mall, Richmond, British Columbia V6X 3T6
www.bcgs.ca

British Isles FHS of Greater Ottawa
PO Box 38026, Ottawa, Ontario K2C 3Y7
www.bifhsgo.ca

England

Cumbria FHS
(covers the present-day county of Cumbria, i.e. the historic counties of Cumberland and Westmorland, the part of Lancashire north of Morecambe Bay, and the former West Riding of Yorkshire parish of Sedbergh)
Ulpha, 32 Granada Road, Denton, Manchester M34 2LJ
www.genuki.org.uk/big/eng/CUL/cumbFHS/

New Zealand

New Zealand Society of Genealogists
P O Box 8795, Symonds Street, Auckland 1035
www.genealogy.org.nz

United States of America

British Isles FHS – USA
(has a Scottish study group)
2531 Sawtelle Boulevard, PMB 134, Los Angeles, CA 90064-3124
www.rootsweb.com/~bifhsusa/

British Isles Genealogical Research Association
(has a special interest group for Scotland)
PO Box 19775, San Diego, CA 92159-0775
www.bigra.homestead.com

International Society for British Genealogy & Family History
PO Box 3115, Salt Lake City, UT 84100-3115
www.isbgfh.org

Select Bibliography

SCOTTISH FAMILY HISTORY

Bigwood, Rosemary, *Tracing Scottish Ancestors* (2001), Glasgow: HarperCollins.

Cory, Kathleen B., *Tracing Your Scottish Ancestry* (2001), 2nd edition, Edinburgh: Polygon.

Ferguson, Joan P.S., *Directory of Scottish Newspapers* (1984), Edinburgh: National Library of Scotland.

Ferguson, Joan P.S., *Scottish Family Histories* (1986), Edinburgh: National Library of Scotland.

Hamilton-Edwards, Gerald, *In Search of Scottish Ancestry* (1983), 2nd edition, Chichester: Phillimore.

Holton, Graham S. and Jack Winch, *Discover Your Scottish Ancestry: Internet and Traditional Resources* (2003), Edinburgh: Edinburgh University Press.

Irvine, Sherry, *Scottish Ancestry* (2003), North Provo: MyFamily.com.

James, Alwyn, *Scottish Roots* (2002), 3rd edition, Edinburgh: Luath Press.

Johnson, Gordon, *Census Records for Scottish Families At Home and Abroad* (1997), 3rd edition, Aberdeen: Aberdeen & North East Scotland Family History Society.

Jonas, Linda and Paul Milner, *A Genealogist's Guide to Discovering Your Scottish Ancestors* (2002), Cincinnati: Betterway Books.

Raymond, Stuart A., *Scottish Family History on the Web* (2002), Bury: Federation of Family History Societies.

Sinclair, Cecil, *Jock Tamson's Bairns: a History of the Records of the General Register Office for Scotland* (2000), Edinburgh: General Register Office for Scotland.

Sinclair, Cecil, *Tracing Your Scottish Ancestors* (2003), Edinburgh: Mercat Press.

Steel, D.J., *Sources for Scottish Genealogy and Family History* (1970), London: Society of Genealogists. (Volume XII in the National Index of Parish Registers series.)

GENERAL FAMILY HISTORY

Chapman, Colin R., *Pre-1841 Censuses & Population Listings in the British Isles* (1998), 5th edition, Dursley: Lochin.

Christian, Peter, *The Genealogist's Internet* (2003), 2nd edition, Richmond: The National Archives.

Herber, Mark, *Ancestral Trails* (2003), Stroud: Sutton.

Humphery-Smith, Cecil (ed.), *The Phillimore Atlas & Index of Parish Registers* (2003), 3rd edition, Chichester: Phillimore.

Gibson, Jeremy & Mervyn Medlycott, *Local Census Listings 1522-1930: Holdings in the British Isles* (2001), 3rd edition (with amendments), Bury: Federation of Family History Societies.

DNA

Cavalli-Sforza, Luigi Luca, *Genes, Peoples and Languages* (2001), London: Penguin.

Hart, Anne, *How to Interpret Your DNA Test Results for Family History and Ancestry* (2002), Lincoln, Nebraska: iUniverse.

Savin, Alan, *DNA for Family Historians* (2000), Maidenhead: Alan Savin.

Sykes, Bryan, *Adam's Curse* (2003), London: Bantam.

Sykes, Bryan, *The Seven Daughters of Eve* (2002), London: Corgi.

SCOTTISH HISTORY AND CULTURE

Personal Names in Scotland (1991), Edinburgh: General Register Office for Scotland.

Scots Kith & Kin (1989), Glasgow: Collins.

Black, George F., *The Surnames of Scotland* (1996), Edinburgh: Birlinn.

Blackie, Lorna, *Clans and Tartans: the Fabric of Scotland* (1998), Rochester: Grange.

Costantino, Maria, *The Handbook of Clans & Tartans of Scotland* (2002), Leicester: Silverdale/Bookmart.

Dennis, M.D., *Scottish Heraldry* (2000), Edinburgh: Heraldry Society of Scotland.

Grimble, Ian, *Clans and Chiefs* (2000), Edinburgh: Birlinn.

Grimble, Ian, *Scottish Clans & Tartans* (2002), London: Bounty/Lomond.

Livingstone, Alastair, Christian W.H. Aikman, and Betty Stuart Hart (eds.), *No Quarter Given: the muster roll of Prince Charles Edward Stuart's army, 1745-46* (2001), Glasgow: Neil Wilson.

Maclean, Fitzroy, *Highlanders* (2000), London: Adelphi.

Martine, Roddy, *Scottish Clan & Family Names* (1992), Edinburgh: Mainstream.

McIan, R.R., *The Clans of the Scottish Highlands* (1986), London: Hamlyn. (First published in two parts in 1845 and 1847.)

McLeod, Mona, *Leaving Scotland* (1996), Edinburgh: National Museums of Scotland.

Moncreiffe of Easter Moncreiffe, Iain, and Don Pottinger, *Simple Heraldry* (1993), Leicester: Promotional Reprint/Bookmart.

Moncrieffe of that Ilk, Sir Iain, *Lord of the Dance* (1986), ed. by Hugh Montgomery-Massingberd, London: Debrett's Peerage.

Munro, R.W., *Highland Clans & Tartans* (1987), London: Peerage.

Nicolaisen, W.F.H., *Scottish Place-names* (2001), 2nd edition, Edinburgh: John Donald.

Ross, David, *Scotland: History of a Nation* (2002), New Lanark: Geddes & Grosset/ Lomond.

Ross, David, *Scottish Place-names* (2001), Edinburgh: Birlinn.

Smith, Donald, *Celtic Travellers: Scotland in the Age of the Saints* (1997), Edinburgh: Mercat Press.

Sutherland, Elizabeth, *The Pictish Guide: A Guide to the Pictish Stones* (1997), Edinburgh: Birlinn.

Whyte, Donald, *Scottish Surnames* (2000), Edinburgh: Birlinn.

Index